JANE CLARKE'S

Bodyfoods

cookbook

JANE CLARKE'S

Bodyfoods

cookbook

Photography by Jess Koppel

CASSELLPAPERBACKS

contents

> 'Cooking...means the knowledge of all herbs and fruits and balms and spices, and of all that is healing and sweet in fields and groves and savoury in meats.'
>
> *John Ruskin (1819–1900)*

introduction

bring Bodyfoods into your life

HEALTHY EATING CAN BE THE KEY TO TRANSFORMING YOUR LIFE: it will give you the energy to think more clearly, to lead a more focused life and thereby to achieve your dreams. I've written this book to help you bridge the gap between eating the foods that you love, purely because they taste good, and those that will help you to gain and maintain health and vitality.

If we and our children are to enjoy lifestyles that maximise our bodies' potential, and that give us energy in the morning, as well as inspired minds in the afternoon, then it is crucial that the food that we pile into our supermarket trolleys or cook in our kitchens excites us. It's no use relying on so-called 'health foods' for your well-being; although they may work for you for a day or two, your body will soon be pining for the foods that it enjoys.

I hope my cookbook will inspire you to adopt delicious and nutritious eating habits that are both easy and achievable. This is a cookbook to be used – keep notes on what works for you. Think about keeping a food and emotion/symptom diary for a week or so, taking note of everything you eat and drink alongside how you're feeling; also answer the question, why are you eating or drinking it? This will provide you with invaluable information as to how you can change and use different ideas, foods and drinks to improve your day. I've kept things simple because you shouldn't have to hunt for hard-to-find ingredients according to my Bodyfoods ethos, nor should you have to spend all day cooking. The recipes, which range from simple, energising breakfasts to snacks that you can carry around with you, from dishes that you can have fun creating with your children to dinner-party delicacies, are therefore all based on ingredients that you can find in your local supermarket or delicatessen. In addition to the recipes, sections devoted to the benefits of drinking water and the therapeutic qualities of herbs and edible flowers will explain how you can stimulate your taste buds while also nurturing and healing your body.

Healthy eating can make you feel physically wonderful. The nutrients that we give our bodies can help to resolve everyday health problems, from feeling down to constipation or a low libido. Each recipe in this book highlights a 'magic ingredient', an ingredient that has a specific health-giving quality. Indeed, the ingredients contained in every recipe have been included with the sole purpose of combining flavour with health-giving properties.

As well as having created dishes that you can enjoy at various times of day, I have also devoted a chapter to explaining how the nutraceutical properties of certain foods can alleviate certain lifestyle-related health problems. Nor does my cookbook stop there: because food cures shouldn't be restricted to a list of beneficial nutrients, in this chapter I have translated my advice into two tasty dishes, and have also suggested other recipes in the book that will similarly assist your body to overcome common, but debilitating problems such as headaches, anaemia and high cholesterol.

Whatever your lifestyle and however you're feeling, my recipes (which have been tried, tested and enjoyed at my lunches and supper parties) should inspire your mind, gratify your stomach, and, above all, provide you with the magic ingredients that your body needs to lead a healthy life.

JANE CLARKE
London, 2000

how to eat

'Your ultimate aim should be to eat in a way which enables you to know when you've had enough. If you acknowledge the messages that your stomach sends to your brain, eating will become enjoyable, at the same time also keeping your body fit and healthy.'

In our low-fat, reduced-this and reduced-that society, many people are frightened by the prospect of eating 'real' foods like full-fat cheese, yoghurt or butter. Because such fears usually revolve around issues of weight, and because we have been wrongly encouraged to believe that 'real' foods are fattening, we often believe that it is healthier to eat reduced-calorie products. Not only is this belief based on a wrong assumption (low-fat foods are frequently full of sugar, while low-sugar foods often contain a lot of fat, with the result that they are still high in calories), but reduced-calorie foods are both less tasty than 'real' foods and also contain inferior ingredients (like chemicals and additives intended to make them taste as much like their 'real' counterparts as possible).

Eating butter, cheese and normal, rather than low-calorie chocolate, is perfectly healthy as long as you understand how you can eat such foods without putting on weight or developing food-related health problems. The secret to gaining this know-how has two strands: learning how foods react within your body, and how your appetite mechanism works. Understanding these issues will enable you to offset the potential downsides of one food with the beneficial qualities of another. Your ultimate aim should be to eat in a way that enables you to know when you've had enough. If you obey the messages that your stomach sends to your brain, eating will become enjoyable, at the same time also keeping your body fit and healthy.

Hunger and satiety

Within the brain's 'appetite centre' in the hypothalamus are areas that recognise hunger and areas that acknowledge satiety (the feeling that you get when your appetite has been satisfied). The signals that your stomach sends to either of these areas dictate whether you feel hungry or full.

Satiety encompasses such physical properties as smell, taste, texture and temperature, as well as the emotional aspects of eating, so the more you enjoy what you eat and drink the greater your degree of satiety. In addition, you'll be less likely to be tempted by inappropriate foods if you feel pleasantly full and contented, a goal that you should strive towards when you sit down to eat.

To start with, you should try to follow four main principles when you are eating:

1 Chew your food thoroughly and eat slowly. Stretch receptors within your jaw respond when you chew, which means that the more you chew and the longer you take to eat a meal the greater your eventual feeling of satiety.

2 Keep your taste buds titillated. Try to stimulate as many different senses as you can by incorporating various tastes, textures and temperatures into a meal. Your senses will register these changes in taste and texture and will send many signals to your brain's satiety centre. Remember that boring and unvaried eating habits will cause you to eat more than your body actually needs. (As I tell my patients, eating the same food over and over again is like constantly having sex in the same position – your body will switch off, not on.) In either case, by keeping your brain and senses stimulated you'll feel deliciously satisfied when you've finished.

3 Concentrate on the eating experience; eating at the same time as you're doing something else – watching the television, for instance – diverts your senses and attention from your food and thus confuses your brain, with the result that messages from your stomach won't reach your brain's satiety centre and you won't feel satisfied when you have finished eating.

4 Remember that physical, as well as sensual factors affect your feeling of satiety. When there is food in your stomach, stretch receptors in your stomach's walls send satiety signals to your brain. Low-fibre foods, like sweets or fatty foods, pass through your stomach very quickly, which means that it doesn't have time to send many messages to the brain's satiety centre; because you won't feel full for long you are likely to eat more. The opposite happens when you eat high-fibre foods such as fresh fruits and vegetables, wholegrain cereals and pulses. Since these foods have thick cell walls they stay in the stomach for longer, swell in the presence of water and consequently send lots of satiety signals to the brain. Therefore the best way to eat high fat and sugary foods is to accompany them with a fibre-provider, such as a hearty portion of vegetables, and to make sure that you don't eat sweet and creamy desserts until there is a substantial amount of fibre in your stomach.

By following these principles you'll be able to enjoy only a small amount of a delicious, high-calorie dish, but will still feel full and contented at the end of your meal.

don't forget the water

'About 65 per cent of an adult's body consists of water, a level that must be topped up constantly if we are to remain healthy and looking youthful.'

About 65 per cent of an adult's body consists of water, a level that must be topped up constantly if we are to remain healthy and youthful-looking. Although our bodies can do without food for some time, we can survive for only a few days if we are deprived of water. Only slightly less seriously, if your body is persistently dehydrated you will succumb to feelings of lethargy, energy swings, poor skin, high blood cholesterol levels, urinary-tract infections such as cystitis and bowel problems like constipation.

We mainly lose water through the skin (the skin's inner layer, the dermis, is made up of 70 per cent water and acts as a natural reservoir). More water is lost when we suffer from bouts of vomiting, diarrhoea or any infection that causes fever. Furthermore, now that most of us live in centrally heated houses, and work in centrally heated and air conditioned offices, more water evaporates through our skin than in the days when such innovations didn't exist.

Another strain on our bodies' water reserves is our modern diet, which contains more salt, additives and sugars than in the past. I have therefore drawn on the flavour-enhancing qualities of herbs and spices for the recipes in this book rather than on salt alone. If you crave the extra flavour of salt, add a little to the dish just before it is served instead of including it out of sheer habit.

Your body needs water to help it flush out waste products, to maintain healthy skin, hair and organs, to produce digestive enzymes, to regulate its temperature (water evaporated through the skin cools it down), as well as to help it absorb essential vitamins, minerals and natural sugars. Food can only provide you with a fraction of its potential benefits without water. Think of food like a dry sponge: it sits in the digestive system unable to do much on its own until water joins it and helps it to swell. The food's water-logged cell walls become progressively weaker as they absorb the water until they eventually burst, releasing nutrients into the body rather like a puffball releasing its spores into the air.

High blood fat (cholesterol and triglyceride) levels can be aggravated by lack of water; without water the fibre in foods such as wholegrains, pulses, oats, fruits and vegetables cannot swell and stimulate the body to produce high-density lipoprotein (HDL), that is, 'good' cholesterol, which picks up low-density lipoprotein (LDL) 'bad' cholesterol, as it travels through the bloodstream before depositing it in the gut, from where it is excreted.

How much should you drink?

Drinking plenty of water can make all the difference to your well-being. Most adults should try to drink 2 to 3 litres (about 4 or 5 pints) of water every day. Although this may sound like an awful lot, if you can meet this target your body will look, feel and stay healthier. People who exercise regularly, as well as pregnant women, should drink even more. Exercise causes the body to lose fluid, which can lead to over-heating, dizziness and tiredness, while the body's fluid requirement increases during pregnancy in order to nourish the foetus, and breast-feeding mothers need to drink extra fluid to enable their bodies to produce milk. Remember that children, who are generally more active than adults, can lose a great deal of water through their skin. As a rough guide, a two-year-old needs to drink at least 500 ml (nearly 1 pint) of water and a three-year-old at least 750 ml (1¼ pints) each day and more during hot weather.

Urine is one of the best guides as to whether you are taking in enough water: it should be pale rather than dark, and you should find yourself going to the lavatory regularly throughout the day. (Although you will initially need to urinate more often as a result of boosting your water intake, your body will learn to process the extra fluid efficiently.) If you wake up during the night bursting to go to the loo, stop drinking a couple of hours before you go to bed to enable your body to rid itself of any excess fluid before you retire for the night.

Remember that if you have a poor appetite or need either to put on weight or to maximise your calorie intake you should not drink large amounts of water at meal times. Although water itself does not disturb the digestion, if you fill up your stomach with water there will be less room to accommodate food. If you have a digestive disorder, like a hiatus hernia or oesophagitis, drinking too much liquid can cause the stomach fluids to leak upwards into the oesophagus, irritating the oesophagus walls and bringing on heartburn. In this case, take small sips of water with your meal to refresh your palate and make up your fluid requirement between meals.

Tap or bottled water?

It is up to you whether the water that you drink comes from a tap or a bottle. Mineral and spring waters are ground waters, which means they fell to earth as rain, seeped through rocks and accumulated in underground pools before being bottled on reaching the earth's surface again. The qualities of water labelled 'natural mineral water' are more rigidly defined and better regulated than those of spring water: the water has to come from a source which is naturally protected and has a constant composition, as well as being free from pollution. Most sparkling water has had carbon dioxide pumped into it, although a small proportion is naturally sparkling; this procedure poses no threat to health and also provides a refreshing alternative to still water. Bottled water is handy to carry around with you, to give your child to take to school or to have to hand on your desk – a good reminder to drink a glass of water an hour.

Some people, however, find the concept of paying for bottled water unnecessary and uneconomical (indeed, at the time of writing, 1 litre (1¼ pints) of tap water in my area costs about 0.06 pence – that's up to a thousand times cheaper than bottled water). In the case against bottled water there is also the cost to the environment incurred by the use of plastics or glass in the packaging and the energy used in transportation to consider. If the taste of tap water puts you off, ask your water supplier to test it for contamination (from old water pipes, for example) or bacterial overgrowth. Remember that water companies have a legal duty to meet safety standards and are generally also committed to making improvements to the palatability of water, particularly in terms of its taste and clarity. A water filter can remove some of the unpleasant tastes of tap water, but if you use one make sure that it is regularly serviced, otherwise you will contaminate your water by passing it through an unclean filter.

Adding zest to water

You can make water look and taste more interesting by adding shavings of fresh root ginger, slices or a squeeze of fresh lemon, a few drops of orange-blossom water or a dash of elderflower or lime cordial. Alternatively, you could mix your water with fruit juice. Water doesn't always have to be served cold – why not use it to make a fruit or herbal tea or tisane? There are many such products on the market, and you can also make your own by infusing some fresh mint or root ginger in boiling water.

Remember, however, that drinks which contain caffeine (tea, coffee, cola-based drinks and hot chocolate) do not count towards your recommended daily intake of 2 to 3 litres (4 to 5 pints) of water, because caffeine is dehydrating. So although you can safely enjoy two or three cups of such drinks a day, make sure that you are drinking plenty of pure water too – it's your best liquid asset.

breakfast time
boosts

1

Despite the saying 'breakfast like a king, lunch like a knave and dine like a pauper', there is no hard-and-fast rule about when, or how much, you should eat. Instead it's a question of understanding how your body responds to food and how you can maximise your well-being through eating. Breakfast provides an invaluable opportunity to enable you to do the latter. A bowl of fresh fruit salad eaten shortly after getting up, for example, will provide a slow release of energy to help you to get through the morning, as well as a good dose of vitamins and minerals. Scrambled eggs on toast, on the other hand, supply a dose of protein that goes towards building up your muscles, which is particularly necessary if you expend a lot of physical energy throughout the day.

Everyone responds differently to food in the morning: some people feel sleepy and unable to function after eating a large breakfast, whereas others need a hearty breakfast before they embark upon the day's activities. Although there is a lot of confusion about the necessity of having breakfast as a result of these differing reactions, it is important to consider the scientific evidence. It has been proved that the body generally performs and feels better if you eat something (however little) between waking up and having lunch. Because you have had to rely on your body's nutrient reserves to keep you going overnight, the morning is the best time to start topping them up again.

Scientific studies have furthermore shown that children who either skip breakfast or eat very little at the beginning of the day are at a disadvantage when compared with those who eat a healthy breakfast. This is because the brains of children who have empty stomachs tend to receive less than the ideal level of blood sugar. Although this doesn't mean that they're likely to keel over at any moment, certain parts of their memories may not work as well as they should, which may cause problems at school. Children who've breakfasted properly generally have better reaction times and are also more proficient at such problem-solving exercises as mental arithmetic (this is most apparent in children with lower IQs).

A well-nourished brain can improve adults' ability to recall information, too, because it has received sufficient fuel (that is, sugar) to enable it to perform effectively. Before you start reaching for a sugar lump, however, you should understand that the sugar = brain-fuel formula is not that simple. For example, if you eat a sugar lump or gulp down a can of sweetened 'sports drink' first thing in the morning when you have an empty stomach, your blood-sugar level will shoot up, consequently stimulating your body to secrete a large amount of insulin (the hormone that transfers sugar from the blood to the body's cells). This insulin reaction will in turn cause your blood-sugar level to plummet, thus leaving your brain with very little sugar to work with.

Instead, the best way in which to deliver sugar to your brain is to package it within a high-fibre, carbohydrate-rich food, such as wholemeal bread, wholegrain cereal, oats or fresh fruit. The fibre contained within such foods helps to slow down the rate at which sugar is both released into the blood and carried to the brain, thereby enabling you to remain focused. The wide range of high-fibre, carbohydrate-rich foods offers you both choice and flexibility at breakfast time.

If time is short in the morning, how about a puréed fruit drink, such as a mango, raspberry and banana smoothie (see page 20)? Smoothies (or puréed fruit drinks) are ideal breakfasts, being both quick to make and containing energising properties. They are also a good way in which to give children a vitamin boost at the beginning of the day. Refreshing and revitalising drinks, they can be made with various combinations of fruits, such as oranges, grapefruits, peaches, apricots and other seasonal fruits, with or without added yoghurt. Try adding a few baked fruits or a spoonful of puréed fruit to smoothies, as these give a slighly different texture. This breakfast can be eaten at home, as well as at the gym after a work-out or after you've arrived at the office.

If your early mornings are not so rushed, relaxing over a wild-mushroom omelette with fresh herbs (see page 31) is a highly effective way in which to prepare yourself for some productive hours thereafter. However, keep in mind that pregnant women and people who have compromised immune systems should avoid eating undercooked and soft-boiled eggs. Although children under the age of eight or nine months can eat cooked egg yolks, egg whites are more challenging to a young gut, so you should wait until your children are a year old before feeding them eggs.

Remember that breakfast doesn't have to be eaten at a set time each day, although you should try to have something within a couple of hours of getting up.

Another good reason why you should eat a little something in the morning is because your digestive system performs much more efficiently if it is allowed to work on a small amount of food every few hours. If you deprive your stomach of food from the evening of one day until the lunchtime of the following day you will expose yourself to two potentially adverse situations. Firstly, because the stomach continually produces acid in the anticipation that this will be needed to help to digest food, if you don't eat anything the consequent build-up of acid may cause indigestion. Secondly, you may reach 'starvation point' and thus become inclined either to eat inappropriately or to over-eat. It is vital that you understand that over-eating after a period of fasting can take your digestive system by surprise. The stomach's production of digestive juices slows down when you haven't eaten for a while, so if you over-eat thereafter there won't be enough juices in your stomach with which to digest the food properly. The undigested food may then either remain in your stomach, making you feel uncomfortable and bloated, or may pass through your digestive system in a partly digested state, which may cause such unpleasant gut problems as diarrhoea or constipation.

In summary, eating something – ideally a high-fibre, carbohydrate-rich food – in the morning assists your body in every respect.

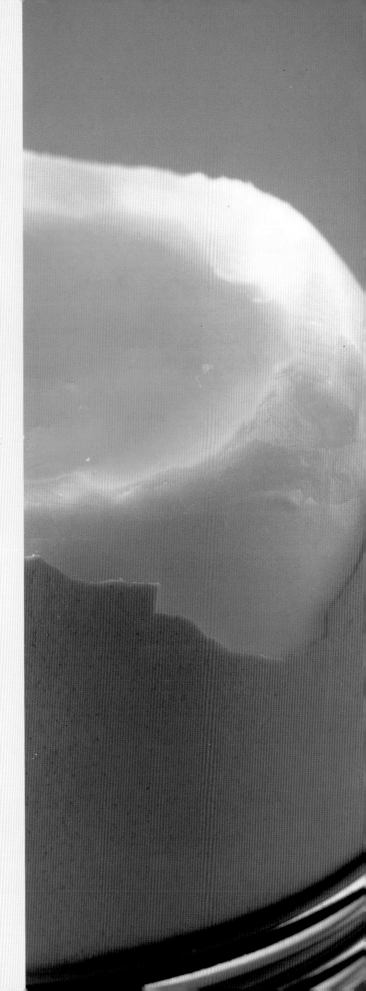

Mango, peach & pink grapefruit smoothie   makes 2 large glasses

magic ingredient... mango

Mango is rich in vitamin C, a nutrient that has wound-healing properties, whether they be post-operative wounds or simply grazed knees. This smoothie is very transportable and could be taken to work or to the gym in a flask.

1 mango, peeled and stoned
1 pink grapefruit, peeled and as much pith removed as possible
1 peach, peeled and stoned
400 g/14 oz low-fat fromage frais or 275 g/10 oz natural yoghurt or 200 g/7 oz cold milk

• Purée all of the ingredients together in a liquidiser until smooth, then chill.

Banana & pineapple energising fruit smoothie   makes 1 large glass

magic ingredient... bananas

Bananas are full of slow-release sugars, so if you have one for breakfast – perhaps in this smoothie – it will sustain your energy levels throughout the rest of the morning. Note that this smoothie can't be kept for long, because after a while the banana will turn grey. In addition, don't keep the smoothie in the fridge, because this can cause the banana to change its chemical composition and thereby cause stomach upsets. It also causes the banana to turn an unappetising grey.

3 bananas
½ fresh pineapple, skinned and core removed
3 tablespoons natural yoghurt

• Purée all of the ingredients together in a liquidiser until smooth and then drink immediately.

Left: Breakfast smoothies

Mango, raspberry & banana smoothie   makes 1 large or 2 small glasses

magic ingredient... bananas

Bananas contain high levels of potassium. Potassium and sodium levels within the body behave rather like a pair of scales: when the potassium level in the blood is high, sodium levels are low. Topping up your potassium intake therefore helps to correct high blood pressure. The combination of pineapple and bananas makes this smoothie rich in slow-release fruit sugars.

1 mango, peeled and stoned
75 g/3 oz raspberries
1 banana
200 g/7 oz low-fat fromage frais, or 150 g/5 oz natural or soya
  yoghurt or 75 ml/3 oz cold milk

• Purée all of the ingredients together in a liquidiser until smooth, then drink immediately.

Blueberry, banana & nectarine breakfast salad   serves 1

magic ingredient... blueberries

Blueberries and nectarines are both rich sources of vitamin C, a strong antioxidant and disease-fighter. Blueberries also contain ellagic acid, which is currently being investigated for anti-cancer properties.

100 g/3½ oz fresh blueberries
1 medium-sized banana, sliced
2 ripe nectarines, sliced

• Combine the blueberries, banana and nectarines in a bowl and serve, perhaps with a dollop of natural yoghurt, custard or porridge.

Banana & peanut butter slices serves 2

magic ingredient... peanut butter

Peanuts contain high levels of zinc, a nutrient that plays a powerful role in building up a strong immune system. Combining nuts (as is also the case with pulses) with a cereal (such as bread) enables the body to receive the correct balance of amino acids, which act as building blocks for healthy muscles and immune systems. This is a great tasting breakfast for children who don't have peanut allergies.

4 slices warm wholegrain toast
2 tablespoons crunchy peanut butter
2 large bananas

- Spread the toast with the peanut butter.
- Slice the bananas on top of the toast and eat immediately.

Iced coffee makes 4 glasses

Magic ingredient... coffee

Coffee causes the body's smooth muscles to relax, which can help to get a lazy (constipated) gut going in the morning. Drinking large quantities of coffee (as well as tea, cola, hot chocolate and some so-called 'energising drinks') is not advisable however, and you should keep your intake down to two or three cups a day. If you would like to increase the fat and calorie content of this drink, you could add a scoop of vanilla ice cream or dollop of fresh cream.

1 tablespoon cocoa
1 tablespoon cold water
1 large mug black coffee, made with freshly ground coffee
600 ml/1 pint cold milk
½ teaspoon vanilla essence
6 ice cubes

- Mix the cocoa and cold water into a smooth paste in a bowl. Add the coffee, milk and vanilla essence.
- Place the liquid and the ice cubes in a blender and whizz for a minute or so, until the ice has been crushed and the ingredients have been well blended.

Marinated oranges   serves 5

magic ingredient... oranges

Oranges are rich in potassium, which helps to reduce fluid retention and also balances high blood pressure by lowering the level of sodium in the body. A high potassium intake can furthermore play a part in regularising an erratic heartbeat (arrhythmia).

10 large oranges, peeled and thinly sliced into rounds
225 g/8 oz caster sugar
finely grated zest and juice of 1 lemon
180 ml/6 fl oz fresh orange juice

- Arrange a third of the orange slices in a single, overlapping layer in a large serving dish. Sprinkle with a third of the sugar and a third of the lemon zest. Repeat twice more until you have used up all of the oranges.
- Combine the lemon juice with the orange juice and pour over the oranges. Cover and refrigerate for at least 6 hours, ideally overnight. Serve chilled.

Melon energiser   serves 4

magic ingredient... melon

Melons contain high levels of fructose, a fruit sugar that gives your body a sustainable, slow-release energy boost. With their powerful energising properties they are therefore an ideal breakfast food to get you going at the start of a hectic day.

2 small, ripe Ogen or Charentais melons, halved and seeds removed
175 g/6 oz large, ripe red or white grapes, halved and seeds removed
1 teaspoon preserved ginger, finely chopped

- Using either a melon-baller or a teaspoon, remove the flesh from the melons and place it in a bowl. Add the grapes and preserved ginger and leave to stand for 30 minutes.
- Meanwhile, trim the bottoms off the melon shells so that they can stand unsupported. Put the shells in a plastic bag and place them in the fridge.
- Once the melon flesh has been well macerated, pile the flesh back inside the melon shells and serve.

Left: Marinated oranges

Porridge with honey & apple purée   serves 1

magic ingredient... apples

Apples are rich in cholesterol-lowering fibre. Remember to drink some water or freshly squeezed fruit juice when eating porridge in order to help your body deal efficiently with the nutrients and fibre that it contains. The size of the cup that you use to measure the ingredients doesn't matter, as long as you get the proportions of oats to water right.

Apple purée

2 large Bramley apples, peeled and cored
juice of ½ lemon
dash of water

Porridge

1 cup porridge oats
2 cups water, milk or a mixture of the two
pinch of salt or brown sugar
1 tablespoon acacia or runny honey (optional)

- Make the apple purée by slicing the apples into a small saucepan and adding the lemon juice and a dash of water. Bring to the boil, then cover and simmer for 10 minutes, or until the apples are soft, stirring occasionally.
- Using either a hand blender or a fork, mash the apple into a soft purée. (The purée can be kept covered in the fridge for a few days.)
- Place the oats, water or milk and salt or brown sugar in a saucepan and bring to the boil, stirring all the time. Simmer for 5–10 minutes (depending on desired texture), continue stirring.
- Gently stir the apple purée (and a little honey, if you prefer a slightly sweeter taste) into the porridge and serve at once.

Fruity oatmeal cereal   serves 4

magic ingredient... oats

Oats are rich in soluble fibre, which helps to keep the body's 'bad' cholesterol levels down. They are also a good source of biotin (also known as vitamin H), the nutrient that is needed to maintain young, healthy-looking skin and to build strength into hair. If you prefer a porridge-type cereal, you could leave it to soak in water overnight. It is also rather delicious frozen. This cereal will stay fresh for two to three days when stored in an airtight container.

225 g/8 oz rolled porridge oats
50 g/2 oz each dried prunes, apricots, dates and pears
2 tablespoons sultanas
2 tablespoons raisins
2 tablespoons chopped dates
4 tablespoons hazelnuts
4 tablespoons wheat germ

- Mix all of the ingredients together. Serve with milk, yoghurt or fruit juice.

Carrot & buckwheat bread   makes a 450 g/1 lb loaf

magic ingredient... buckwheat flour

Buckwheat flour is a gluten-free starch that helps to give the body energy
without aggravating gluten-sensitive digestions. It is suitable for people
who suffer from coeliac disease or allergies and sensitivities to gluten.

100 g/3½ oz carrots, grated
150 ml/5 fl oz water or milk
1 egg
100 g/3½ oz buckwheat flour
100 g/3½ oz rice flour
1 teaspoon bicarbonate of soda
½ teaspoon cream of tartar
¼ teaspoon tartaric acid
pinch of salt
25 g/1 oz caster sugar
1 tablespoon vegetable oil

- Preheat the oven to 220°C/425°F/gas mark 7.
- Liquidise the grated carrots, milk and egg. Mix all of the dry
  ingredients together and fold into the carrot purée with the oil.
- Grease and line a 450 g/1 lb loaf tin with baking parchment
  and pour in the batter.
- Bake in the oven for 35 minutes, or until a skewer inserted into
  the centre of the loaf comes out clean.
- Remove from the oven and cool for a few moments before
  turning out on a cake rack to cool completely

Banana soft bread   makes a 450 g/1 lb loaf

magic ingredient... tartaric acid

The inclusion of tartaric acid in this recipe helps to give the bread a good
texture, a quality that is frequently lacking in gluten-free bread like this,
since it is gluten that forms the strong bread structure. Tartaric acid can
be bought from pharmacies in large tubs, but if you cannot find it you
could use extra cream of tartar instead.

1 large banana
110 g/4 oz tofu
1 egg
150 ml/5 fl oz milk
150 g/5 oz rice flour
50 g/2 oz cornflour
25 g/1 oz soya flour
1 teaspoon bicarbonate of soda
1 teaspoon cream of tartar
½ teaspoon tartaric acid
pinch of salt
1 teaspoon sugar
1 tablespoon olive oil
50 g/2 oz sesame seeds

- Preheat the oven to 190°C/375°F/gas mark 5.
- Liquidise the banana, tofu, egg and milk in a blender.
- Combine the rice flour, cornflour, soya flour, bicarbonate of
  soda, cream of tartar, tartaric acid, salt and sugar and fold into
  the banana purée with the olive oil.
- Grease and line a 450 g/1 lb loaf tin with baking parchment
  and pour the batter into it. Sprinkle the sesame seeds over the
  top and bake in the oven for 35 minutes, or until a skewer
  inserted into the centre of the loaf comes out clean.
- Remove from the oven and cool for a few moments before
  turning out on a cake rack to cool completely

Vine-ripened tomatoes on toast   serves 1

magic ingredient... tomatoes

Tomatoes are rich in a very powerful anti-cancer nutrient called lycopene. Men in particular should aim to eat ten portions of tomato-based foods (even if contained in a Bloody Mary) every week, in order to reduce by 45 per cent the risk of developing cancer of the prostate gland. The olive oil furthermore increases the level of 'good' cholesterol in the blood.

2 slices wholemeal bread
2–3 vine-ripened tomatoes, sliced
drizzle of olive oil
salt and freshly ground black pepper

- First toast the wholemeal bread.
- Place the tomatoes on top of the toast and drizzle a little olive oil over them. Finally, season to taste.

Boiled egg with toasted flat bread   serves 1

magic ingredient... flat bread

Flat bread is low in fibre, which means that it can be easily digested by people who have delicate digestive systems. It can be found in supermarkets and delicatessens. It is delicious when toasted with a little butter and perfect for dunking into a soft-boiled egg. If you can't find it however, thick slices of toasted wholegrain bread make a good alternative to flat bread.

1 egg
1 or more slices flat bread or wholegrain bread
butter

- Place the egg in boiling water for between 3 and 10 minutes, depending on how soft you like your eggs. If the egg is for a pregnant woman or someone who has a problem with their immune system however, boil it for 5 to 10 minutes.
- In the meantime, toast the flat or wholegrain bread, spread it with butter and then serve with the egg.

Left: Vine-ripened tomatoes on toast

Brown soda bread   makes a 450 g/1 lb loaf

magic ingredient... bicarbonate of soda

The inclusion of bicarbonate of soda in this recipe enables the dough to
rise and the bread to taste wonderful without the use of yeast, which can
aggravate the symptoms of people who suffer from such yeast sensitivities
as candidiasis.

450 g/16 oz wholemeal flour (organic if possible)
1 heaped teaspoon bicarbonate of soda
1 teaspoon salt
1 teaspoon Demerara sugar
25 g/1 oz butter
500–600 ml/16–20 fl oz buttermilk

- Preheat the oven to 230°C/450°F/gas mark 8.
- In a large bowl, mix together all of the dry ingredients, rubbing
  in the butter lightly. Make a well in the centre and add about
  500 ml/16 fl oz of the buttermilk. Working with a knife from
  the centre, gather up the mixture to make a soft, wet dough
  (you may have to add more buttermilk to make the mixture
  'sticky wet').
- Grease a 450 g/1 lb round or oblong loaf tin, spoon in the
  dough and bake in the oven for 30 minutes.
- Cover the top of the loaf with greaseproof paper and bake for
  a further 10 to 15 minutes.
- Turn the loaf out on to a wire rack and cover it with a clean tea
  towel. Leave it to cool slightly before slicing the bread.

John's bread   makes a 450 g/1 lb loaf

magic ingredient... wholemeal flour

Wholemeal flour contains high levels of fibre, which helps to protect
against heart disease by reducing the levels of 'bad' cholesterol in the
blood. If you are overweight, fibre-rich foods also help you to slim.

350 g/12 oz strong unbleached white flour (organic if possible)
50 g/2 oz wholewheat flour
50 g/2 oz bran
1 heaped teaspoon bicarbonate of soda
1 teaspoon salt
1 teaspoon Demerara sugar
25 g/1 oz butter
500–600 ml/16–20 fl oz buttermilk

- Preheat the oven to 230°C/450°F/gas mark 8.
- Mix together all of the dry ingredients, rubbing the butter in
  lightly. Make a well in the centre and add about 500 ml/16 fl
  oz of the buttermilk. Working with a knife from the centre,
  gather up the mixture to make a soft, wet dough (you may
  have to add more buttermilk to make the mixture 'sticky wet').
- Grease a 450 g/1 lb round or oblong loaf tin, spoon in the
  dough and bake in the oven for 30 minutes.
- Cover the top of the loaf with greaseproof paper and bake for
  a further 10 to 15 minutes.
- Turn out the loaf on to a wire rack and cover it with a clean tea
  towel. Leave it to cool slightly before slicing the bread.

Kedgeree   serves 4–6

magic ingredient... fish

Fish contains high levels of tryptophan, an amino acid that helps the brain
to produce the endorphins (or 'happy hormones') serotonin and
noradrenaline. There can be few better ways to begin a leisurely day than
by tucking into this sustaining and delicious dish.

1 large Finian or natural-smoked haddock
milk or water
175 g/6 oz long grain rice, preferably basmati
2 blades mace
75 g/3 oz butter
2 hard-boiled eggs, chopped
salt and freshly ground black pepper
1 raw egg, beaten
at least 6 tablespoons single cream
2–3 tablespoons fresh parsley, chopped

- Poach the haddock in just enough milk or water to cover it, drain and set aside. Rinse the rice and boil it with the mace until tender. Drain well.
- Heat two-thirds of the butter in a sauté pan and flake the haddock into it. Stir for a few minutes. Mix in the rice and, when it is piping hot, add the hard-boiled eggs. Adjust the seasoning if necessary.
- Take the pan off the heat and add the raw egg, cream, the rest of the butter and enough parsley to give a speckled effect.
- Taste the kedgeree and add extra cream if you like. Turn out onto a warm dish and serve at once on warm plates.

Wild mushroom omelette with fresh herbs   serves 1

magic ingredient... eggs

Eggs, particularly the yolks, are packed with vitamins and minerals. The vitamin D that they contain, for example, works in conjunction with calcium to produce strong, healthy bones and teeth. When eggs are used in omelettes they make excellent, high-protein, muscle-building breakfasts. Note however, that young children, pregnant women and older people should avoid eating omelettes because there is a slight risk that uncooked eggs could cause salmonella poisoning. For safety reasons, it is also better to buy wild mushrooms rather than picking them yourself.

25 g/1 oz butter
about 125 g/4 oz wild mushrooms, chopped
salt and freshly ground black pepper
fresh herbs, such as tarragon or parsley, chopped (optional)
3 eggs

- Heat half of the butter in a small saucepan and then sauté the mushrooms for a couple of minutes. Add a little seasoning and some herbs, if you like. Remove the pan from the heat.
- Meanwhile, break the eggs into a bowl and beat them lightly with a fork. Place the remaining butter in an 18–20 cm/7–8 in omelette pan over a high heat. As soon as the butter begins to foam, add the beaten eggs and cooked mushrooms and leave for about 10 seconds.
- Using the back of a spoon, stir the omelette mixture lightly and then tip it on to a warmed plate (the omelette should be creamy in the centre). Serve at once.

Left: Wild mushroom omelette with fresh herbs

long and
short lunches

Lunches have changed a great deal over the past fifty years. Gone are the days when we stopped work for a couple of hours and went home to tuck into the substantial main meal of the day. By contrast, today it's more often a question of making a quick dash to the sandwich shop and then hastily consuming our purchase while working, or perhaps worse still, having a couple of mouthfuls of the children's left-overs, followed by a quick cup of coffee and a chocolate biscuit. For many of us, taking the time to have lunch seems like too much of an indulgence, one that we save for the weekend when we can afford the time and can also cope better with the sleepy feelings that we frequently experience when our stomachs are full.

If we choose the foods that suit our bodies, lunch should provide the perfect opportunity to supply ourselves with nutritional, energising fuel. Yet many people don't like to take a food break in the middle of the day because they end up feeling far from energised, instead wanting to crawl into bed for a catnap. Because we lead demanding, highly stressed lives, we want and need to feel alert, not sleepy, during the afternoon. What many of us don't realise however, is that the type of food that we eat, as well as the manner in which we eat it, influence how we feel. For instance, pasta, bread and other starchy foods encourage the brain to produce sleep-inducing hormones. It does this because these foods need to be digested slowly, which means that the stomach and digestive system (which is, after all, a muscle) require oxygen to perform their duties efficiently. The brain therefore secretes hormones that encourage us to sleep in order to diminish both our desire and physiological ability to divert oxygen from our stomach to our limbs to enable us to rush around. If we ignore the effect of these hormones however, and instead command our limbs to move energetically, oxygen is diverted from the stomach, which frequently leads to indigestion, stomach cramps and bloating. In short, the brain's response to these starchy foods is one that is conditioned by physiological efficiency.

If you have time to take a siesta after lunch, perhaps at the weekend, then by all means go ahead and make a dish like my pasta with courgettes and lemon (see page 51) or baby potatoes topped with guacamole and roasted peppers (see page 51); eating these foods and then having a little snooze is the best way to allow your body to enjoy and digest them. If you don't have the time, however, choose a protein-, fruit- and vegetable-based lunch in which the proportion of vegetables, fruits and/or protein is high, such as my asparagus and lemon

salad (see page 42), a bowl of my courgette and pea soup (see page 38) or a chunk of cheese with some figs, grapes and crisp, green celery. By opting for such foods your body's hormonal response will encourage, not hinder your desire to be energetic in the afternoon.

There is an further benefit of having a protein-rich lunch, too. Proteins are made up of amino acids, two of which, L-phenylalanine and tryptophan, encourage the body to produce endorphins (mood-enhancing hormones). Eating a protein-rich lunch, like my sea bass with crab (see page 48), chicken Caesar salad (see page 45) or some lean charcuterie with cherry tomatoes, therefore not only helps to prevent the mood swings that may occur mid-afternoon, but also enables your body's blood-sugar levels to remain more constant (which means that you shouldn't experience 'sugar dips' at 4 pm). If eating protein-rich foods doesn't appeal to you, having a fruit- or vegetable-based lunch, like a bowl of soup followed by some fruit, can similarly energise your body.

I hope that this chapter will encourage you to reconsider your usual lunchtime choices. If you are organised and a little eclectic in terms of your ideas, you can turn lunch into an interesting affair, rather than settling for the 'which sandwich bores me least?' option. Practicality is usually a big issue, which is why sandwich bars may initially appear to be your only resort as a convenient source of lunch, but why not make a large cauldron of soup or a tray of grilled vegetables at home at the weekend to take to work in small plastic containers and then heat them up in the microwave at work (if your office has one)? Alternatively, if for reasons of either practicality or preference, bread is your staple food for lunch, remember that you don't have to stick to the traditional sandwich made up of two slices of sliced bread with something in the middle. Many

different, mouth-watering types of breads are readily available today, such as ciabatta, focaccia or flat bread, which you can either make into wraps or warm up and eat with dips and crudités; muffins, too, can be topped or filled with lean, protein-rich foods and salads. In order to vary its texture and taste, you could also toast some bread to serve with a bowl of hearty soup, while an open focaccia sandwich will show off its topping in a gloriously sensory-stimulating manner.

Browse through this chapter, make a list of ingredients and ideas and then turn lunch into a delightful, energising interlude in the middle of what would otherwise be a hectic, draining day. Half an hour or so is plenty of time in which to eat something nutritious and delicious, and taking a break will also allow you to step back from your busy routine for a while and refresh both your body and mind. Remember, too, that if your lunch is going to do wonders for you, you need to drink plenty of water (see pages 12–13) to enable your body to absorb the beneficial nutrients contained in your food; it is these that will dictate how you'll feel for the rest of the afternoon.

Focaccia with chargrilled peppers & ham   serves 4

magic ingredient... focaccia

The focaccia in this quick-to-make, satisfying sandwich contains olive oil, which in turn contains monounsaturated fats that boost the levels of the 'good' form of cholesterol, high-density lipoprotein (HDL), within the blood. High HDL levels can help ward off heart attacks, strokes and circulation problems.

crunchy grain mustard
4 slices focaccia bread
2 red or yellow peppers, sliced
2 beef tomatoes
4 slices lean, honey-roasted ham

- Preheat the grill to a high heat.
- Lightly spread a little grain mustard over the focaccia slices.
- Place the peppers and tomatoes, skin side uppermost, under the hot grill to brown or char. Leave them to cool.
- Divide the peppers and tomatoes between the four slices of focaccia and top with the ham.

Roasted aubergine & pepper wrap   serves 4

magic ingredient... red pepper

Red peppers are rich in betacarotene, a powerful antioxidant that is converted into vitamin A within the body. It is vital for promoting growth, healthy skin and hair, keen eyesight and strong tooth enamel.

2 large aubergines
1 red pepper
2 cloves garlic, finely chopped
juice of 2 limes
3 tablespoons tahini (sesame-seed paste)
¼ teaspoon ground cumin
salt and freshly ground black pepper
2 flat breads, warmed and sliced in half lengthwise
50 g/2 oz spinach leaves

- Preheat the oven to 220°C/425°F/gas mark 7.
- Roast the aubergines and pepper for about 30 minutes, until they are charred and soft. Allow them to cool and then slit open the aubergines, scoop out the flesh and place it in a bowl. Add the garlic, lime juice, tahini, cumin and a little salt and pepper. Mash the ingredients with a fork until the paste is smooth.
- When it is cool, remove the skin from the pepper. Slice the pepper and set it aside.
- To serve, spread the aubergine paste over the flat breads and top with the roasted pepper and spinach. Roll up the flat breads and cut them in half before serving.

Left: Focaccia with chargrilled peppers and ham

Celery soup   serves 6

magic ingredient... celery

Celery plays an important role in reducing fluid retention, a common
pre-menstrual symptom that can cause many women to feel uncomfortable
and to gain weight before their periods start.

dash of olive oil
1 medium-sized onion, chopped
1 clove garlic, finely chopped
1 large bunch celery, trimmed and thinly sliced (reserve the
   leaves for garnishing)
900 ml/1½ pints vegetable or chicken stock
1 large potato, peeled and diced
2 tablespoons fresh basil, torn
salt and freshly ground black pepper
dash of cream, natural yoghurt or crème fraîche (optional)

• Heat the olive oil in a medium-sized pan. Add the onion, garlic
  and celery and sauté for about 10 minutes, or until the
  vegetables start to soften. Pour in the stock, add the diced
  potato, bring to the boil, cover and simmer for 15 minutes.
  Allow the soup to cool.
• Blend the cooled soup in a liquidiser or blender. Stir in the torn
  basil and season to taste.
• If you want a slightly creamy taste, add a dash of cream,
  natural yoghurt or crème fraîche to each bowl of soup before
  serving. Garnish with the reserved celery leaves.

Courgette & pea soup   serves 6

magic ingredient... courgettes

Courgettes contain high levels of magnesium, which enables the body to
absorb and metabolise other essential minerals, including calcium, that the
body needs in order to build strong bones and teeth. The powerful
interaction between magnesium and calcium therefore plays a role in
preventing osteoporosis.

dash of olive oil
4 small courgettes, chopped into small pieces
1 small onion, sliced
900 ml/1½ pints fresh chicken stock
225 g/8 oz fresh or frozen peas
25 g/1 oz fresh basil, torn
salt and freshly ground black pepper

• Heat the olive oil in a medium-sized pan. Add the courgettes
  and onion and sauté for about 10 minutes, or until the
  vegetables start to soften. Pour in the stock, bring to the boil
  and simmer for 15 minutes.
• Add the peas to the soup and simmer for a further 5 minutes.
  Leave the soup to cool.
• Blend the soup in a liquidiser or blender and stir in the basil.
  Season to taste and serve immediately.

Jerusalem artichoke soup   serves 4

magic ingredient...artichokes

Artichokes are very easy to digest and a nourishing food, making this soup
ideal for people who suffer from digestive problems. Garlic is furthermore
rich in allicin, which helps to raise the levels of high-density lipoprotein
(HDL), 'good' cholesterol, within the blood.

8 cloves garlic, in their skins
400 g/14 oz Jerusalem artichokes, peeled and chopped
150 g/5 oz potatoes, peeled and diced
2 small onions, roughly chopped
3 sticks celery, roughly chopped
1 sprig lemon thyme
2 teaspoons caster sugar
500 ml/16 fl oz vegetable stock, ideally fresh
juice of 1 lime
2 tablespoons fromage frais
salt and freshly ground black pepper
grated zest of 2 limes
2 tablespoons natural yoghurt

- Preheat the oven to 190°C/375°F/gas mark 5.
- Place the garlic cloves in a small roasting tin and roast them in the oven for 20 minutes. When cool enough to handle, pop them out of their skins.
- Place the artichokes, potatoes, onions, celery, roasted garlic, lemon thyme and 1 teaspoon of caster sugar in a large saucepan. Add the stock and bring to the boil. Simmer for about 20 to 25 minutes, or until the artichokes are tender.
- Remove the pan from the heat and add the lime juice and fromage frais. Season to taste with a little salt and pepper and then liquidise the soup until it becomes smooth.
- Mix the lime zest, yoghurt and remaining sugar together. Set aside.
- Reheat the soup gently, being careful not to let the fromage frais curdle. If it does, remove the pan from the heat and add about 2 teaspoons of cornflour mixed with a little water and then liquidise the soup again; you should find that this solves the problem.
- Serve the soup with a dollop of the lime yoghurt on top.

Roasted butternut squash soup   serves 4

magic ingredient... butternut squash

The slow-release carbohydrates contained in the butternut squash
encourage the body to produce calming hormones, thus making this soup
excellent for de-stressing both the mind and body. Roasting the butternut
squash before you make the soup really brings out its nutty flavour.

Croûtons
*2 thickly cut slices wholewheat or granary bread, crusts
  removed and cut into cubes*

Soup
*900 g/2 lb butternut squash, peeled, de-seeded and chopped
  into large chunks
dash of olive oil
1 onion, finely chopped
1 clove garlic, finely chopped
3 saffron strands steeped in a tablespoon hot water or
  ½ teaspoon turmeric
600 ml/1 pint chicken or vegetable stock
salt and freshly ground black pepper
8 tablespoons thick natural yoghurt or cream*

- To make the croûtons, preheat the oven to 200°C/400°F/gas mark 6 or preheat the grill to a high heat. Arrange the cubes on a greased baking sheet and toast the cubes until they are brown on all sides. Set aside.
- To make the soup, preheat the oven to 220°C/425°F/gas mark 7. Place the butternut squash chunks on an oiled baking sheet and roast for about 25 minutes, until the edges are golden brown and their flesh is soft to the touch.
- In a large saucepan, heat the olive oil and sauté the onion and garlic for about 10 minutes, until translucent. Add the steeped saffron or turmeric and cook for 1 minute, stirring constantly.
- Add the roasted butternut squash chunks to the onion mixture and stir for a couple of minutes. Pour in the stock, bring to the boil and simmer for 20 minutes, stirring occasionally.
- Cool and then tip the soup into a liquidiser, blend until smooth and season to taste. Add the yoghurt or cream and heat gently to bring the soup to serving temperature (do not let it boil). Sprinkle with freshly ground black pepper and croûtons.

Bean & curly kale soup   serves 6

magic ingredient... beans

Beans assist the body to regulate and stabilise its reproductive hormones,
particularly oestrogen and progesterone, which help reduce the severity
of menopausal symptoms. Fresh herbs, like sage, can help to calm an
irritated digestive system, making this soup soothing and easy to digest.

*4 large cloves garlic, finely chopped
1 tablespoon olive oil
350 g/12 oz soaked and cooked cannellini or borlotti beans
1.5 litres/2½ pints vegetable stock
2 heaped tablespoons tomato purée
6 fresh sage leaves
225 g/8 oz curly kale, stems removed
salt and freshly ground black pepper
juice of 1 lemon
Parmesan cheese, freshly grated*

- In a large saucepan, sauté the garlic in the olive oil for 30 seconds. Add half of the soaked and cooked beans and a dash of the vegetable stock.
- Purée the rest of the beans in a blender with the tomato purée, the rest of the stock and the sage leaves. Stir the puréed bean mixture into the saucepan. Chop up the kale finely and add it to the soup. Simmer for 30 minutes.
- Just before serving, season to taste, add the juice of 1 lemon and sprinkle with a little freshly grated Parmesan cheese.

Left: Roasted butternut squash soup

Asparagus & lemon salad   serves 2

magic ingredient... lemon

The lemon contained in the citron confit used in this salad is rich in vitamin C, which, like the folic acid in the asparagus, assists the body to absorb iron and other essential nutrients. Folic acid is particularly important during pregnancy and also plays a role in preventing iron-deficiency anaemia, as well as heart disease. The citron confit (lemon preserved in filtered water, fleur de Siel and herbs, available from specialist delicatessens) has a wonderfully concentrated flavour, which means that you only need to use a thin slither.

1 large bunch asparagus, washed and trimmed
150 g/5 oz fresh or frozen broad beans
1 ripe avocado
2 heads of chicory, washed and outside leaves removed
⅛ citron confit, thinly sliced, or the juice of 1 lemon
dash of olive oil
juice of 1 lemon
salt and freshly ground black pepper

- Steam the asparagus and broad beans until they are *al dente*. Plunge them into cold water immediately to cool them quickly and then drain well.
- When they are cool enough to handle, remove the skins from the broad beans to reveal their bright green hearts.
- Peel and stone the avocado, then cut it into thin slices.
- Separate the leaves from the chicory heads and arrange them on a serving plate with the beans, asparagus and avocado slices.
- Arrange the citron confit slices or sprinkle the lemon juice over the salad ingredients. Drizzle the salad with a little olive oil and lemon juice. Season the salad to taste and then toss it gently to ensure that the dressing is evenly distributed.

English salad with home-made salad dressing   serves 2

magic ingredient... carrots

We are so frequently seduced by Mediterranean produce that it's easy to
ignore the fresh English salad ingredients, like carrots, which are rich in
such antioxidants as betacarotene, an anti-ageing nutrient.

4 eggs
2 large clumps broccoli
100 g/3½ oz fresh broad beans
100 g/3½ oz runner beans, de-strung, sliced into small pieces
70 g/2½ oz fresh peas
2 medium-sized carrots, scrubbed, sliced into small pieces
6 radishes, scrubbed, sliced into small pieces
2 spring onions, topped and tailed
3 tomatoes, sliced into quarters
selection of rocket and Little Gem lettuce leaves
2 cooked beetroots, sliced into small pieces
2 tablespoons mixed fresh marjoram, thyme, basil and parsley,
   finely chopped, to garnish

Salad dressing
1 shallot, finely diced
1½ tablespoons red wine vinegar
¼ teaspoon salt
5–6 tablespoons olive oil

- Boil the eggs for 5 minutes, until the whites are hard but the
  yolks are still a little soft. Cool them quickly in cold water,
  remove shells and then cut them in half.
- Steam the broccoli, broad beans, runner beans and peas until
  they are al dente (cooked but still firm). Cool them quickly in
  cold water and drain well.
- Arrange all of the salad ingredients on a bed of salad leaves on
  a serving plate, leaving the beetroot till last and positioning it
  carefully to avoid its colour leaching out into the other
  ingredients.
- Make the salad dressing by placing the shallot, vinegar and salt
  in a bowl and then gradually whisking in the olive oil to make
  an emulsion. Taste the mixture, if necessary adding more
  vinegar or oil, depending on how tart you want the salad
  dressing to be.
- Drizzle a little of the dressing over the salad ingredients on the
  platter to coat them lightly and then sprinkle them with the
  fresh herbs. Serve the rest of the salad dressing separately, in a
  ramekin dish.

Avocado and palm heart salad   serves 2

magic ingredient... avocados

Avocados are rich in vitamin E (which the body needs if it is to develop
and maintain strong cells, especially in the blood) and vitamin B complex
(which is essential for the development of a healthy nervous system). Palm
hearts are the hearts of palm tree shoots from the West Indies; they can
be bought tinned from delicatessens, but if you can't find them use
asparagus instead.

1 head chicory, washed and outside leaves removed
40 g/1½ oz rocket
2 avocados, peeled, stoned and sliced
1 tin palm hearts or asparagus, drained
⅛ citron confit, thinly sliced, or the juice of 1 lemon
dash of olive oil
salt and freshly ground black pepper

- Separate the leaves from the chicory heads and arrange them
  with the rocket on a serving plate. Place the avocado slices and
  palm hearts or asparagus on top of the leaves.
- Arrange the citron confit or sprinkle the lemon juice over the
  salad and drizzle with olive oil. Season with salt and plenty of
  freshly ground black pepper.

Salad niçoise   serves 4

magic ingredient... tuna

The tuna (as well as anchovies) in this dish contains high levels of protein,
which helps to ensure that your muscles remain healthy and also raises
your energy levels. Rich in beneficial fish oils, it furthermore diminishes
the risk of developing heart disease.

75 g/3 oz broad beans
handful of leaves from the heart of a lettuce
6 vine-ripened tomatoes
3 hard-boiled eggs, cut into quarters
450 g/1 lb fresh seared tuna, roughly flaked
8 tinned anchovy fillets, drained of their oil
16 black olives

Dressing
4 tablespoons olive oil
1 tablespoon white wine vinegar
1 clove garlic, crushed
2 tablespoons fresh parsley, chopped
1 teaspoon pickled capers, rinsed
salt and freshly ground black pepper

- Blanch the broad beans and leave them to cool.
- Divide the lettuce leaves between 4 plates. Cut the tomatoes into quarters and add them to the lettuce leaves, along with the eggs, tuna and beans.
- Mix the dressing ingredients together and pour the dressing over the salads. Toss the salads gently. Lay 2 anchovy fillets over each salad and scatter 4 olives over the top.

Swiss chard with lime dressing   serves 4

magic ingredient... chard

Chard is rich in vitamin C, which helps the body to fight colds and
infections, and in iron, which acts against fatigue and prevents anaemia.
Women, children and people who have ulcers all need to ensure that their
iron intake is generally high.

900 g/2 lb Swiss chard
juice of 2 limes
4 tablespoons olive oil
salt and freshly ground black pepper

- Prepare the chard by tearing the leaves apart and washing thoroughly. (If you are using large leaves, remove the central stalks; if you are using young, small leaves, retain the stalks.) Mix the lime juice with 3 tablespoons of the olive oil and season to taste.
- Heat the remaining olive oil in a saucepan, add the chard and stir. Cover and allow to cook for 5 minutes. Remove the lid and stir again. Add the lime mixture and mix well. Serve iimmediately.

Chicken Caesar salad   serves 3–4

magic ingredient... chicken

Chicken is a lean source of tryptophan, an essential amino acid that encourages the brain to produce serotonin, a 'happiness hormone'; it also contains easily digestible protein. It is safer not to serve this dish to young children, pregnant women or older people, because there is a slight risk that the raw egg yolks it contains may cause salmonella poisoning.

1 medium-sized Cos or crisp-hearted lettuce
3 roasted chicken breasts, thinly sliced
1 avocado, peeled and sliced or cubed
2 tablespoons fresh tarragon leaves, torn

Garlic croûtons
2 cloves garlic, crushed
3 tablespoons olive oil
3 slices white bread, crusts removed and cut into cubes

Caesar dressing
2 medium-sized eggs
6 tablespoons olive oil
juice of 1 small lemon
1 tablespoon Worcestershire sauce
salt and freshly ground black pepper
25–50g/1–2 oz Parmesan cheese, freshly grated

- Remove the lettuce leaves from the lettuce stalks – use only the tender central leaves. Wash and dry the leaves and place in a plastic bag in the fridge until they are needed.
- To make the croûtons, stir the garlic into the olive oil and leave to infuse for as long as possible. In a pan, heat the garlic oil (but do not let it burn) and sauté the bread cubes until they are an even golden colour. Drain well on kitchen towels.
- To prepare the Caesar dressing, first plunge the eggs into boiling water, bring the water back to the boil and then boil for 1 minute. Break the eggs into a large salad bowl, scraping out the thin layer of cooked egg white. Gradually whisk in the olive oil and then the lemon juice, Worcestershire sauce, salt and pepper. Add the lettuce leaves, croûtons, sliced chicken breasts, avocado and ⅔ of the Parmesan cheese.
- Toss the salad lightly. Divide it between 3 or 4 large plates, sprinkle each with the remaining cheese and tear some fresh tarragon leaves over the top. Serve immediately.

Vine tomato & walnut salad   serves 4

magic ingredient... tomatoes

Tomatoes contain the anti-cancer nutrient lycopene. Men in particular (who have a risk of developing prostrate cancer) should therefore try to eat ten tomato-rich meals or snacks every week, like this tomato salad, or even just tomato sauce or tomato juice.

450 g/1 lb ripe vine tomatoes, sliced
50 ml/2 fl oz olive oil
25 ml/1 fl oz walnut oil
1 clove garlic
1 tablespoon fresh basil, torn
1 tablespoon fresh flat-leaved parsley, chopped
salt and freshly ground black pepper

- Arrange the tomato slices on a flat dish.
- Liquidise the olive oil, walnut oil, garlic, basil and parsley to make a dressing. Season to taste and pour the dressing over the tomatoes. Serve immediately.

Baby vegetables with a lime & walnut dressing   serves 4

magic ingredient... walnut oil

Walnut oil contains high levels of vitamin E, which plays an important role
in reducing the incidence of heart disease. For best results, steam the
vegetables in a steamer which has two or three levels.

Dressing

6 tablespoons walnut oil
¼ teaspoon white truffle or sesame oil
1 tablespoon honey
2 tablespoons lime juice
salt and freshly ground black pepper

Baby vegetables

225 g/8 oz whole baby (new) potatoes, cleaned
225 g/8 oz baby carrots, cleaned
110 g/4 oz whole baby parsnips, cleaned
225 g/8 oz baby courgettes, with flowers still attached
225 g/8 oz runner beans, topped and tailed
110 g/4 oz whole baby leeks, cleaned
110 g/4 oz broad beans

- Make the vegetable dressing by mixing all of the dressing
  ingredients together (an easy way to do this is to shake them
  together in a screw-topped jar).
- Bring a large pan of water to the boil and add the potatoes to
  the water. When the potatoes have been boiling for 6 minutes,
  place a Chinese steamer over them and pop the carrots and
  parsnips into the bottom level, nearest the steam. After more 2
  minutes add the courgettes to the carrots and parsnips. Place
  the remaining vegetables in the top level of the steamer. Cook
  for a further 3 to 5 minutes, until all of the vegetables are
  cooked. Note that a colander placed over a large pan of water
  with a saucepan lid on top will also work as a steamer.
- Place the vegetables on a serving plate and drizzle the dressing
  over the top, to taste.

Plum salad   serves 4

magic ingredient... plums

Plums contain potassium, a nutrient which helps to alleviate fluid
retention by reducing the levels of sodium in the body.

1 orange
1 curly endive (frisée)
3 plums, stoned and quartered
2 peaches, stoned and cut into 8 wedges
1 small fennel bulb, cut into slices
1 bunch flat-leaved parsley, stems removed
freshly ground black pepper
20 roasted hazelnuts, skins rubbed off

Dressing

2 tablespoons hazelnut oil
½ teaspoon tarragon mustard
1 teaspoon tarragon-flavoured white wine vinegar
1 teaspoon sugar
grated zest and juice of ½ a lime

- Finely grate the zest of the orange. Using a long, sharp knife,
  cut the orange into 4 slices, holding the orange over a plate to
  collect the juice. Remove and discard the orange peel.
- To make the dressing, place the hazelnut oil, mustard, the juice
  collected when segmenting the orange, vinegar, sugar, orange
  zest, lime zest and juice in a liquidiser or blender and liquidise
  until smooth.
- Pull off the small leaves of the curly endive and mix them with
  the plum and peach pieces, sliced fennel and flat-leaved parsley.
- To serve, place a slice of orange on to each plate. Toss the salad
  in the dressing, season with black pepper and pile on to each
  orange slice. Sprinkle with the hazelnuts and serve at once.

Left: Baby vegetables with a lime and walnut dressing

Sea bass with crab   serves 4

magic ingredient... sea bass

Sea bass is a rich source of tryptophan, an essential amino acid that helps to boost energy levels and the brain's production of mood-enhancing hormones such as serotonin.

Prawn, cucumber and tarragon salsa

2 tablespoons tarragon-flavoured white wine vinegar
1 tablespoon sugar
1 teaspoon Dijon mustard
1 tablespoon olive oil
4 sprigs tarragon, leaves removed and chopped
100 g/3½ oz cucumber, seeds removed and diced
40 g/1½ oz peeled prawns
1 small red onion, diced
2 tomatoes, skinned, de-seeded and diced
salt and freshly ground black pepper

Fish and crab topping

4 sea bass fillets, each 175 g/6 oz, skinned and cut in half
100 g/4 oz white crab meat
4 tablespoons wholemeal breadcrumbs
1 bunch chives, finely chopped
1 small egg, beaten
salt and freshly ground black pepper
1 tablespoon olive oil
500 g/1 lb 2 oz baby spinach, washed and drained
1 lemon, halved

- To make the salsa, first mix the vinegar with the sugar and mustard. Add the olive oil, tarragon, cucumber, prawns, onion and tomatoes. Season to taste with salt and pepper, cover and refrigerate for at least 1 hour.
- Preheat the oven to 200°C/400°F/gas mark 6. Run your fingers over the sea bass fillets to make sure that all of the bones have been removed; if you find any, pull them out with tweezers.
- Mix the crab meat with the breadcrumbs, chives and egg and season to taste. Spread half of the crab meat mixture over 4 pieces of sea bass. Place the other fillets on top and spread them with the remaining crab mixture. Transfer to a non-stick baking sheet and bake in the oven for 15–18 minutes.
- Heat a large, heavy-bottomed saucepan over a high heat. Add the olive oil and spinach and cover with a lid. Cook for 1 to 2 minutes, stirring regularly, or until the spinach is cooked. Season with salt and pepper and then drain.
- Transfer the spinach to 4 warmed plates and place the sea bass on top. Arrange a little salsa around the outside of the plates and squeeze the lemon halves over the sea bass.

Braised fennel   serves 1

magic ingredient... fennel

Fennel helps to settle a disturbed digestive system by reducing stomach acidity, as well as wind and colic pain.

1 fennel bulb
dash of olive oil
salt and freshly ground black pepper
Parmesan cheese, freshly grated

- Preheat the oven to 190°C/375°F/gas mark 5.
- Trim a thin slice from the base of the fennel bulb and remove the tough outer leaves, reserving fronds for garnish. Cut the bulb in half and place cut side down in a gratin dish. Drizzle over a little olive oil, season and cover the dish with foil.
- Place dish in the oven for 20–30 minutes, until fennel is soft.
- Remove from the oven, discard the foil and scatter over a little Parmesan cheese. Place under a hot grill for 5 minutes, until the cheese has melted and the fennel has turned golden brown. Garnish with the reserved fennel fronds and serve.

Spinach eggy bread   serves 8

magic ingredient... spinach

An iron-rich vegetable, spinach can help your body to maintain healthy
blood and muscles. If your iron intake is insufficient, you may suffer from
iron-deficiency anaemia, particularly if you don't eat much red meat.

700 g/1½ lb fresh or frozen spinach
50 g/2 oz wholemeal breadcrumbs
110 g/4 oz strong Cheddar cheese, grated
6 medium eggs, beaten
110 g/4 oz feta cheese, softened
110 g/ 4 oz cottage cheese
50 g/2 oz Parmesan cheese, freshly grated
1 tablespoon olive oil
½ teaspoon grated nutmeg
salt and freshly ground black pepper

- Preheat the oven to 180°C/350°F/gas mark 4.
- If you are using fresh spinach, wash thoroughly, then drain well.
  Remove the stems and steam for about 10 minutes, or until it is
  soft. Drain well, making sure that you remove all of the excess
  water (let it cool slightly and then press it with your hands). If
  you are using frozen spinach, defrost and then squeeze out the
  excess water. Chop the spinach roughly.
- Set aside 25 g/1 oz of the breadcrumbs and 25 g/1 oz of the
  Cheddar. In a large bowl, mix the spinach with the rest of the
  ingredients.
- Lightly oil a 23 x 33 cm/9 x 13 in baking tray. Dust the bottom
  of the tray with the reserved breadcrumbs and spread the
  spinach mixture over the top. Sprinkle with the reserved
  Cheddar and place the baking tray in the oven for 45 minutes
  to 1 hour, or until the topping is golden brown and firm. Serve
  straight from the oven.

Oatcakes   makes 6

magic ingredient... oats

Oats are rich in soluble fibre and contain less gluten than wheat, making
them easier for people with gluten sensitivities to digest. The molasses in
these pancake-like oatcakes furthermore provide the body with an iron
boost; if you can't buy molasses, use Muscovado sugar instead.

50 g/2 oz oat flour
175 g/6 oz porridge oats
pinch of salt
¼ teaspoon bicarbonate of soda
50 g/2 oz butter
50 g/2 oz molasses or Muscovado sugar

- Preheat the oven to 190°C/375°F/gas mark 5.
- Mix the oat flour, porridge oats, salt and bicarbonate of soda
  together. Melt the butter and molasses or Muscovado sugar in
  a saucepan over a low heat, add them to the dry ingredients
  and mix well.
- Drop 6 well-spaced spoonfuls of the oatcake mixture on to a
  greased baking tray and bake in the oven for 10 minutes, or
  until the oatcakes are firm. Remove the oatcakes from the oven
  and cool them on a cake rack.

Pasta with courgettes & lemon   serves 4

magic ingredient... pasta

As well as being quick to cook, pasta is a very comforting and settling food. This piquant dish is ideal if you suffer from indigestion, if you're pregnant or if you're just a little headachy or nauseous and want something simple to prepare and eat.

4 courgettes, sliced
3 tablespoons olive oil
1 clove garlic, crushed
450 g/1 lb pasta bows or other pasta shapes
1 teaspoon citron confit
3 tablespoons roasted pine nuts
salt and freshly ground black pepper
Parmesan cheese, freshly grated

- Place the courgettes in a colander and sprinkle them with salt to draw out any excess water. Leave for 30 minutes, then rinse with cold water and pat dry.
- Heat the oil in a large pan and sauté the garlic. Add the courgettes and sauté for a further 5 minutes.
- Meanwhile, boil the pasta until it is *al dente*. Drain well.
- Tip the pasta into the frying pan, mix well, add the citron confit and pine nuts, season and sprinkle with Parmesan cheese before serving.

Baby potatoes with guacamole & roasted peppers   serves 2

magic ingredient... avocado

Avocados are very addictive fruits that are also rich in beneficial oils and vitamin E, which is good for the skin and hair. Using avocados as a topping for the potatoes provides a dairy-free sauce that both moistens the potatoes and complements the peppers. The peppers furthermore contain betacarotene, a nutrient that helps to prevent heart disease.

12 baby (new) potatoes
1 red pepper
1 green pepper
salt and freshly ground black pepper

Guacamole
1 ripe avocado, mashed
1 teaspoon fresh lemon or lime juice
1 large clove garlic, crushed
4 drops hot chilli sauce (such as Tabasco)
¼ teaspoon each salt and freshly ground black pepper

- If you are cooking the potatoes in the oven, first preheat the oven to 200°C/400°F/gas mark 6. Bake in the oven for 20–30 minutes, or until they are soft in the centre when tested with a fork. If you are using a microwave oven, microwave the potatoes on full power for about 7 minutes.
- Meanwhile, grill the peppers under a hot grill until they have browned, turning during the grilling process to ensure that they are evenly coloured. When cool enough to handle, remove the skins, stalks and seeds and slice them up. Set aside.
- Mix all of the ingredients for the guacamole together. After you have made the guacamole, remove the potatoes from the oven. Holding the potatoes in a kitchen towel, carefully slice them in half and arrange on a serving dish. Pile the guacamole on top of the potato halves, decorate with the peppers and season to taste.

Left: Pasta with courgettes and lemon

Chargrilled vegetable pizza makes 2 large pizzas

magic ingredient... vegetables

The vegetables contained in this pizza topping are rich in fibre and betacarotene, powerful nutrients that hinder free-radical damage within the body, thereby lessening the risk of developing cancer and also preserving the skin's collagen and elastin fibres.

Pizza dough
350 g/12 oz strong wholemeal flour
1 sachet instant, easy-blend yeast
1 teaspoon salt
210 ml/7 fl oz warm water
1 tablespoon olive oil

Tomato sauce
1 tin chopped tomatoes
2 cloves garlic, peeled and sliced
1 tablespoon tomato purée
salt
1 tablespoon fresh herbs such as oregano, basil and marjoram, chopped

Topping
1 aubergine, sliced
2 courgettes, sliced
1 bunch asparagus spears
200 g/7 oz buffalo mozzarella, drained and sliced
16 black olives
dash of olive oil

- Make the dough by sieving the flour into a bowl. Add the yeast and salt. Mix well and add the warm water (it should be warm and not hot, otherwise the extreme heat will kill the yeast). Add the olive oil. Mix the ingredients together with your hands until the dough forms a ball and leaves the side of the bowl.
- Place a little flour on your hands and then transfer the dough to a floured flat surface and knead it, pushing, pulling and mixing it well with your hands to combine all of the ingredients together and enable the yeast to distribute itself evenly within the dough. Knead for 10 minutes, until the dough is smooth.
- Put the dough in a floured bowl, cover and place it in a warm place for 1½ hours, or until it has doubled in size.
- Meanwhile, make the pizza sauce by first tipping the tomatoes into a bowl. Add the garlic, tomato purée, salt, herbs and a dash of olive oil and mix together. Set sauce aside.
- Chargrill the aubergine, courgettes and asparagus spears until they are soft. Place to one side.
- When you are ready to cook the pizza, preheat the oven to 230°C/450°F/gas mark 8. Lightly grease a baking tray. Knock back the pizza dough (knock all of the air bubbles out of it) by placing the dough on a floured board and kneading it vigorously for a couple of minutes. Then divide the dough into two and press out each piece into a pizza shape.
- Place the pizza bases on the baking tray and spread 1 tablespoon of the tomato sauce over each. Top with the chargrilled vegetables, sliced mozzarella and olives. Place the pizzas in the oven for about 15 minutes, or until the bases are golden brown and the cheese has melted. Drizzle a little olive oil over the top before serving.

Roasted pepper, onion & courgette pizza   serves 8

magic ingredient... onions

The onions in this pizza contain high levels of anti-bacterial agents, which help the body to keep colds at bay. As well as incorporating lots of varied tastes and textures, this pizza will therefore give your immune system a delicious boost.

Pizza dough
225 g/8 oz white flour
225 g/8 oz wholemeal flour
25 g/1 oz fresh yeast, dissolved in 2 tablespoons warm milk
1 teaspoon salt
300 ml/10 fl oz warm water
dash of olive oil

Tomato sauce
35 g/1½ oz butter or a dash of olive oil
1 onion, thinly sliced
1 carrot, thinly sliced
1 clove garlic, crushed (optional)
900 g/2 lb tomatoes, skinned, de-seeded and chopped
2 tablespoons fresh basil, torn
1 teaspoon sugar (optional)
salt and freshly ground black pepper

Topping
2 red or yellow peppers, roughly chopped
3 courgettes, thickly sliced
1 large onion, thinly sliced
dash of olive oil
200 g/7 oz buffalo mozzarella, thinly sliced
½ teaspoon fresh sage, finely chopped
salt and freshly ground black pepper
Parmesan cheese shavings

- To make the pizza dough, sift the white and wholemeal flour into a mixing bowl and make a well in the middle. Pour the dissolved yeast into the well, then add the salt and mix the ingredients together with your fingers. Gradually add the warm water (make sure that it is not too hot, or it will kill the yeast), kneading until the dough is light, smooth and very elastic.
- Divide the dough into 4 balls, cover and leave them to rise in a warm place for about 1 hour (the dough should double in size).
- To make the tomato sauce, first melt the butter or heat the olive oil in a saucepan. Add the onion and carrot (and garlic, if you are using it) to the pan and cook for about 5 minutes, or until the vegetables have softened. Add the tomatoes, basil, sugar (if you need it to bring out the flavour of the tomatoes) and season to taste. Simmer for 15 minutes, or until the tomatoes have become mushy. Set the tomato sauce aside.
- In the meantime, preheat the grill to a high heat. Place the peppers, courgettes and onion on a baking tray and drizzle a little olive oil over them. Grill the vegetables under the hot grill until their skins start to turn brown and then set them aside.
- Preheat the oven to 225°C/425°F/gas mark 7.
- On a floured surface, roll out the pizza dough to form 4 circles of 30 cm/12 in and place them on 2 greased baking sheets. Spread the tomato sauce over the pizza bases and then arrange the grilled vegetables and slices of mozzarella over them. Sprinkle with sage, salt and pepper. Place the pizzas in the oven for 15 to 20 minutes.
- Sprinkle shavings of Parmesan cheese over the top and serve immediately.

Raspberry yoghurt   serves 4–6

magic ingredient... raspberries

Raspberries contain high levels of the anti-ageing nutrient vitamin C.
Although it's better to use fresh raspberries, you could use frozen ones
out of season, but steer clear of tinned raspberries because they
frequently contain either sugar and/or additives. You could serve this
dessert either in wine glasses or brightly coloured bowls, decorated with
a few fresh raspberries and mint leaves. Another idea is to serve it with a
flapjack to add a little crunch.

275 g/10 oz fresh raspberries
225 g/8 oz plain fromage frais
110 g/4 oz Greek-style yoghurt

- Reserve a few raspberries to use as a garnish and then liquidise
  the remaining raspberries in a food processor. Strain the purée
  through a sieve to remove the seeds.
- Combine the fromage frais and yoghurt and then stir the purée
  into the yoghurt mixture, making sure that the ingredients are
  well mixed.
- Pour into glasses or bowls, chill and garnish with fresh
  raspberries before serving.

Ginger and pear fluff   serves 6

magic ingredient... egg yolks

Eggs contain every essential amino acid that your body needs to build
healthy muscles. Contrary to popular belief, the cholesterol in eggs does
not produce 'bad' cholesterol in the blood. This recipe may seem a little
fiddly, but the result is well worth the effort. When whisking the
ingredients together you can use an electric or a balloon whisk (I prefer
the latter). If you are using an electric whisk, remember to take care
when whisking over the heated saucepan.

75 g/3 oz preserved ginger in syrup
4 egg yolks
50 g/2 oz caster sugar
100 ml/3 fl oz pear eau-de-vie or pear liqueur

- Drain the syrup off the ginger and then chop the ginger very
  finely.
- Half fill a large saucepan (it needs to be large enough to hold
  the base of a mixing bowl without touching the water) with
  cold water. Put all of the ingredients into a mixing bowl and
  whisk them together. Place the mixing bowl into the saucepan
  and heat the water over a moderate heat (make sure that the
  water doesn't boil – the temperature should be below
  90°C/194°F, otherwise the egg will start to cook). Whisk the
  egg mixture for 12 minutes, until it turns shiny and frothy and
  resembles half-beaten egg whites.
- Serve in small glasses.

Grapefruit & orange mousse   serves 4

magic ingredient... grapefruit

Grapefruit contains high levels of bioflavonoids, powerful antioxidants that are concentrated in the peel and that boost the immune system's ability to resist developing cancer and heart disease.

3 oranges
1 grapefruit
juice of 1 lemon
4 egg whites
50 g/2 oz white caster sugar
3 tablespoons water
mint leaves

- Grate the zest from 1 orange. Peel the 3 oranges and grapefruit and separate them into segments, removing any pith. Set a few segments aside for decoration.
- Put the fruit segments into a saucepan with the lemon juice and cook gently for 15 to 20 minutes, or until they have become soft. Leave to cool and then mash them together.
- Beat the egg whites until they form peaks. Put the sugar and water into a small saucepan and simmer gently for 5 minutes, or until all of the sugar has dissolved. Leave to cool for 10 minutes.
- Add the egg whites to the liquid sugar and mix well. Allow the egg mixture to cool completely before blending it into the cold fruit mixture.
- Divide the mousse between four plates and decorate with the reserved fruit segments.

Creamy prunes   serves 4

magic ingredient... prunes

Prunes are packed with antioxidants, the nutrients that assist the body to build barriers against disease. They are also an excellent short-term cure for constipation, either in prune juice or in this indulgent dessert. Remember when making this dish that they need to be soaked overnight.

400 g/14 oz prunes
600 ml/1 pint red wine
2 small sachets vanilla sugar
200 g/7 oz white cheese, preferably ricotta or lebneh

- Soak the prunes overnight in just enough water to cover them.
- Drain the prunes reserving 890 ml/30 fl oz of water. Set aside 4 prunes for decoration.
- Place the red wine, vanilla sugar and prunes in a pan and cook gently for 30 minutes.
- Drain the prunes (reserving the cooking liquid), cool them and then remove the stones. Place the prunes and their liquid in a food processor or liquidiser and purée until the mixture is smooth. Add this mixture to the reserved prune water and stir until it becomes very creamy. Chill the mixture in the fridge.
- Before serving, divide the prune mixture between four small bowls and decorate with the white cheese and one prune per bowl. Alternatively, blend in the cheese when you cream the prune mixture and serve in small bowls.

snacks and quick fixes

People often feel guilty about snacking between meals, maybe because many traditional snacks, like biscuits and crisps, aren't generally considered to be the healthiest of foods. Yet even these snacks can provide health benefits if they are eaten correctly and not to excess. Crisps, for example, may contain vitamin C, while biscuits may be made with oats or wholemeal flour, both of which are fibre-providers. Even shortbreads made with white flour can provide a valuable non-dairy source of calcium (white flour having been fortified with this nutrient in Britain since the Second World War). Although snacking can provide your body with health-giving nutrients, it all too often consists of picking at inappropriate foods that leave you feeling worse half an hour later.

Indeed, you may already be familiar with the blood-sugar level crashes that are caused by eating chocolate bars, or else you may suffer from indigestion after consuming a packet of crisps or from the bloating that results from drinking a fizzy beverage. Successful snacking depends on knowing what best to eat, as well as when, and how, to eat it

You probably already know that eating too many high-fat, high-sugar snack foods can cause weight gain and an irritated gut, as well as mood and energy swings. The best way in which to ensure that snacks help, rather than hinder, your body to function effectively is to opt for those that contain beneficial nutrients. One such nutrient is fibre, a woody substance found in the cell walls of plants that aids the body to absorb the other nutrients contained in the snack in a controlled fashion. A biscuit made with wholemeal flour, my date and chocolate cake (see page 70) and apricot and oat honey muffins (see page 71), or a sandwich made with wholegrain bread, will produce slow, but sustainable increases in your blood-sugar and energy levels. A drink made from freshly squeezed fruits, such as my raspberry and blueberry smoothie (see page 63), will give you the right sort of sugar 'fix' rather than an instant, but short-lived, boost, because when in the presence of water (see pages 12–13) the fibre in the fruits has a cushioning effect on the body's absorption of sugar. Keeping the amount of fat and sugar that you consume on the moderate, rather than high side will also help you to control your weight better, so try to eat a high-fibre snack like my fresh fruit and yoghurt layers (see page 65) instead of a low-fibre chocolate bar. Another quick fix, slow-release snack you might try are my oatcakes topped with a pure fruit spread or with peanut butter. The oats are rich in

fibre, and also contain biotin, which acts to prevent hair loss, brittle nails and dermatitis.

An important reason why you shouldn't feel guilty about snacking is that you may have the sort of body that feels less tired and more efficient when you have a number of small meals rather than a few large ones. One of the benefits of eating snacks often is that they prevent you from becoming ravenous, which means that your digestive system will be less overloaded when you do eat a larger meal. In addition, eating nutritious snacks between meals helps to keep your blood-sugar levels constant, which means that your brain and muscles receive a steady supply of energy, as a result of which you'll feel in a sunny frame of mind, bursting with energy and able to tackle the tasks of the day.

If your digestive system is deprived of food for long periods of time it may start to slow down its production of digestive juices, which means that when you do eventually eat a meal, your stomach will be ill-prepared to deal with the food that has just arrived in it. It will therefore remain in your stomach until enough digestive juices have been produced to break it down, a scenario that can leave you feeling uncomfortably full, prone to indigestion and basically uncomfortable. Eating a little something every three to four hours will therefore keep your digestive system active.

There is a big difference between snacking and picking at food. Picking is something that you tend to do when you're not concentrating on your food, with the result that your brain won't receive the necessary signals from your stomach to tell your body when to stop eating. Furthermore, most food is far too delicious to pick at. When snacking, you should therefore take the time to sit down and to focus on and enjoy your food. Not only will you enjoy the eating experience more, but by nurturing your body in this way it will feel satisfied and you will consequently feel ready to continue with your daily tasks.

Think about the many nutritious snacks that you can eat, and plan ahead. The following are just a few ideas to inspire you to snack healthily.

- Make sure that you have a plentiful supply of fruit at work.
- Make a snack at home to take to the office.
- Give your children a slice of home-made cake to eat on the school bus to help them resist the high-fat convenience snacks that will inevitably tempt them in local shops.
- Snack on some high-fibre foods, like my apricot and oat honey muffins, at work before you go to the gym – the fibre that they contain will prevent post-training energy crashes.
- A few oatcakes with a little cheese, eaten while sitting down listening to the messages on your answering machine, will remove the temptation to raid the fridge as soon as you get home from work, only to regret it later when faced with your evening meal.
- Once again, remember to drink plenty of water throughout the day.

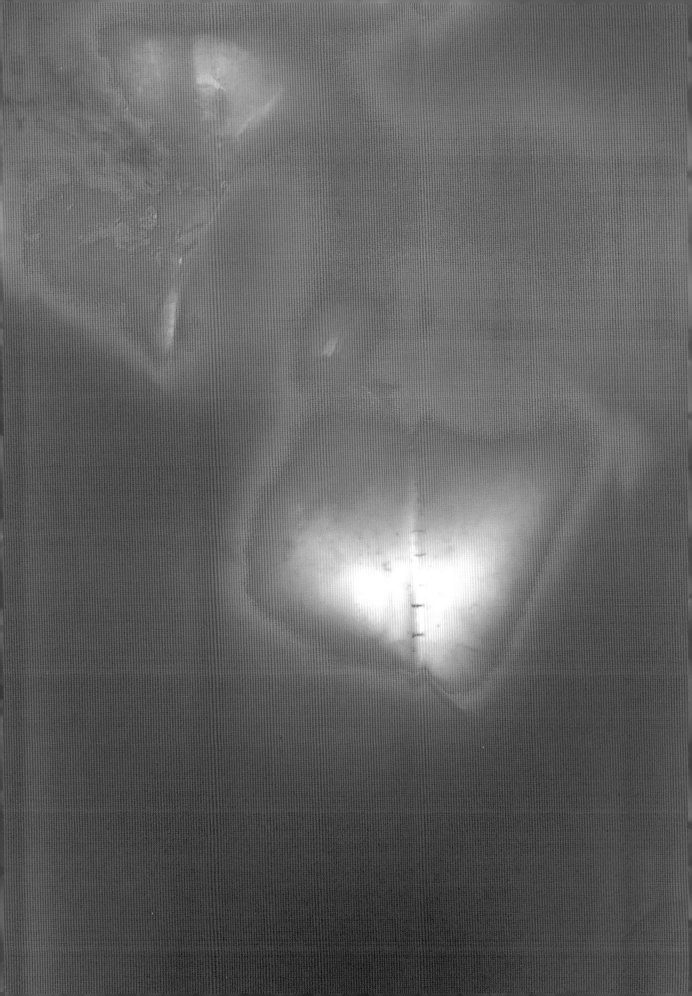

Cranberry zester   makes 4 glasses

magic ingredient... cranberry juice

Cranberries can help to ward off such bladder infections as cystitis,
because the hippuric acid that they contain has the power to repel *E. coli*
bacteria that may settle in the urinary tract and then infect it. It is best
to opt for unsweetened cranberry juice.

300 ml/½ pint cranberry juice
235 ml/8 fl oz cloudy apple juice
1 tablespoon cider vinegar
1 cinnamon stick
2 cloves
2 strips lemon zest
600 ml/1 pint carbonated mineral water, chilled
4 ice cubes

- Place the cranberry juice, apple juice, vinegar, cinnamon stick, cloves and lemon zest in a large saucepan. Bring to the boil and then remove from the heat. Cover the pan and allow it to stand for 1½ hours.
- Strain the juice into a jug and fill it with the chilled mineral water, adding the ice cubes. Serve chilled.

Left: Cranberry zester

Apple mint tea   makes 4 large glasses

magic ingredient... mint

Mint plays an active role in calming the digestion and can also reduce the production of wind. This cold tea is a refreshing and aromatic alternative to many commercially produced, sugar-laden drinks. The Ceylon tea complements the mint with its delicate, nutty flavour.

3 tablespoons fresh mint leaves
zest of 1 lemon
2 Ceylon tea bags
600 ml/1 pint boiling water
400 ml/15 fl oz unsweetened apple juice
juice of 1 lemon
20 ice cubes
4 sprigs mint
4 slices lemon

- Place the mint leaves, lemon zest and tea bags in a warmed china teapot and pour the boiling water over the top. Leave the tea to infuse for 20 minutes.
- Remove the tea bags and pour the tea into a serving jug. Add the apple juice, lemon juice and 10 ice cubes. Place the remaining ice cubes in four glasses and pour over the iced tea. Garnish with the mint sprigs and lemon slices.

Lime & lemon drink   makes 12 glasses

magic ingredient... lemons

Lemons (and limes) are rich in vitamin C, making this drink a useful nutritional precaution for warding off colds, as well as one that refreshes the palate. Vitamin C also promotes the growth of body tissue and speeds up the healing of wounds.

8 lemons
1.5 litres/2½ pints boiling water
4 tablespoons root ginger, peeled and finely grated
110 g/4 oz caster sugar
strained juice of 4 limes
6 lemon slices
12 ice cubes
1.5 litres/2½ pints cold, sparkling mineral water

- Thinly pare the zest from 1 lemon, taking care not to include the white pith. Place the zest in a heatproof jug, pour the boiling water over the top and add the ginger and sugar. Stir well, cover and leave to stand for 1 hour.
- Meanwhile, squeeze the juice from the lemons and strain it into a serving jug. Add the lime juice and leave to stand for 5 minutes. Strain the ginger-and-lemon liquid into the lime-and-lemon juice and stir.
- Add the lemon slices, ice cubes and mineral water to the jug. Serve chilled.

Raspberry & blueberry smoothie   makes 2 glasses

magic ingredient... raspberries

Raspberries contain high levels of vitamin C, an antioxidant whose qualities include cancer prevention. This smoothie is a delectable way of enjoying one of the five portions of fresh fruit and vegetables that you should have each day.

250 g/9 oz raspberries
250 g/9 oz blueberries
1 small pot yoghurt

• Blend all of the ingredients together in a blender or liquidiser until smooth and then pour into 2 glasses.

Strawberry & banana smoothie   makes 1 large glass

magic ingredient... bananas

Bananas contain fructose (fruit sugar), which means that either eating them or drinking them in a smoothie like this one gives your body a slow, but long-lasting energy boost. If you want, you could add a couple of tablespoons of natural yoghurt, milk or fromage frais to the smoothie after the strawberries and bananas have been puréed. Drink the smoothie immediately if possible, otherwise the bananas will turn it brown.

1 small punnet strawberries, washed and hulled
2 large bananas, peeled

• Place the strawberries and bananas in a blender or liquidiser and blend until smooth. Drink immediately.

Fresh fruit & yoghurt layers   serves 4

magic ingredient... yoghurt

This attractive-looking dish is both easy to make and nutritious. The
yoghurt in it contains high levels of calcium, the bone-building and
maintaining nutrient. For their part, the berries are rich in vitamin C,
a powerful antioxidant that helps the body defend itself against colds.

225 g/8 oz strawberries, washed and sliced
225 g/8 oz raspberries, washed
225 g/8 oz blackberries, washed
1 large pot natural Greek-style yoghurt

- Cover the bottom of a glass bowl with a layer of mixed fruit
  and then add a couple of tablespoonfuls of yoghurt. Carry on
  building up layers of fruit and yoghurt until the bowl is full,
  placing a single piece of fruit in the centre of the final layer of
  yoghurt.
- Chill the dish in the fridge before serving.

Left: Fresh fruit and yoghurt layers

Blackcurrant cake   serves 6–8

magic ingredient... blackcurrants

Blackcurrants contain lots of iron, the nutrient that helps to keep your hair healthy and well nourished and acts against fatigue. They are packed with vitamin C which helps the body to absorb iron. It is best to use fresh blackcurrants, but you could use tinned ones out of season.

175 g/6 oz fresh blackcurrants or a 290 g/10 oz tin of tinned blackcurrants
50 g/2 oz brown sugar
2 teaspoons cinnamon
¼ teaspoon nutmeg
175 g/4 oz wholemeal flour
1 teaspoon baking powder
1 teaspoon bicarbonate of soda
50 g/2 oz butter
110 g/4 oz caster sugar
1 teaspoon vanilla essence
210 ml/2½ fl oz sour cream
2 eggs, beaten

- Preheat oven to 180°C/350°F/gas mark 4. Grease a round 20 cm/8 in cake tin and line with greaseproof paper.
- Blend the blackcurrants into a pulp (if you are using tinned blackcurrants, drain off the juice first). Add the brown sugar, cinnamon and nutmeg to the blackcurrants and mix until smooth. Set aside.
- Sift the flour, baking powder and bicarbonate of soda together. In another bowl, cream the butter and sugar together. Add the vanilla essence, sour cream and eggs to the butter mixture and blend well. Gradually beat the flour into the butter mixture, incorporating lots of air.
- Pour the batter into the prepared cake tin and carefully place the blackcurrant mixture on top (it will then sink through the batter mixture).
- Bake for 1 hour; test to see whether it is cooked – it should be springy to the touch. Turn out the cake on to a rack to cool.

Date & orange cake   makes 8 large slices

magic ingredient... dates

The dates, oranges and wholemeal flour are full of fibre and sugars that are released into the body slowly, thereby inhibiting dramatic swings in energy. A slice of this cake provides an energising and a sustaining snack.

50 g/2 oz butter
50 g/2 oz brown sugar
1 teaspoon baking powder
125 g/4 oz plain wholemeal flour
1 teaspoon cinnamon
1 teaspoon ground nutmeg
½ teaspoon ground cloves
4 medium eggs
½ teaspoon vanilla essence
zest and juice of 1 large orange
125 g/4 oz dates, chopped
50 g/2 oz walnuts, chopped

- Preheat the oven to 190°C/375°F/gas mark 5.
- Cream the butter and sugar together. In a bowl, sift together the baking powder, flour, cinnamon, nutmeg and cloves. Gradually beat in the eggs (if the mixture begins to curdle, add a spoonful of the flour). Fold the flour into the mixture. Mix in the vanilla essence, orange juice and zest. Add the dates and walnuts and blend well.
- Grease and line a 23 cm/9 in square cake tin with baking parchment. Pour the batter into the tin and bake for 50 minutes (test to see if it is ready by inserting a cake skewer into the centre, which should come out clean).
- Turn out the cake on to a rack to cool.

Fig & hazelnut tart   serves 6

magic ingredient... figs

Figs are rich in calcium, a vital nutrient in the prevention of osteoporosis, as well as blood-sustaining iron; they also have a mildly laxative effect. Try to buy dried figs that have not been dipped in sugar.

Pastry
25 g/1 oz toasted hazelnuts, ground in a food processor
175 g/6 oz plain white flour
1 teaspoon salt
2 tablespoons soft brown sugar
75 g/3 oz unsalted butter, chilled
2 tablespoons chilled water

Filling
225 g/8 oz dried figs, stems removed and cut into quarters
juice and zest of 1 orange
3 large eggs
110 g/4 oz mascarpone cheese
juice of 1 lemon
1 tablespoon plain white flour
110 g/4 oz soft brown sugar
2 oz/50 g toasted hazelnuts, chopped

- Preheat the oven to 200°C/400°F/gas mark 6.
- First make the pastry by mixing together the ground hazelnuts, flour, salt and sugar. Chop the butter into small pieces and rub it into the flour mixture until the mixture resembles breadcrumbs. Add the chilled water and gently knead the mixture into a moist, but not wet, dough. Wrap in plastic wrap and chill for 1 hour.
- Mix the figs with the orange juice and zest and leave to soak for 30 minutes. Strain the juice from the figs and set it aside.
- In a separate bowl, beat the eggs with the mascarpone cheese, lemon juice, flour and the juice from the figs. Beat in the sugar.
- Roll out the dough and use it to line a round 23 cm/9 in flan tin. Arrange the figs on top of the dough. Pour over the mascarpone mixture and sprinkle the hazelnuts on top.
- Bake the tart at 200°C/400°F/gas mark 6 for 10 minutes, then turn the temperature down to 180°C/350°F/gas mark 4 and bake for a further 20 to 30 minutes, or until the filling has set.

Lemon & poppy seed cake   serves 8

magic ingredient... almonds

Almonds contains high levels of calcium, which helps the body to build strong bones and teeth. Calcium also plays a part in reducing hypertension, making this a good snack if you have high blood pressure.

3 lemons
225 g/8 oz butter
225 g/8 oz caster sugar
3 medium eggs, beaten
25 g/1 oz ground almonds
225 g/8 oz plain white flour
1 teaspoon baking powder
2 tablespoons black poppy seeds

- Preheat the oven to 190°C/375°F/gas mark 5.
- Zest the lemons and set aside. Prepare 12 lemon segments (or as many as the lemons have) by cutting away the lemon skin with a sharp knife and then slicing the lemon as close to the pith as possible to release the segments.
- Cream the butter and sugar together to make a light mixture. Gradually add the beaten eggs to the mixture, blending them in well. Fold in the lemon zest and segments, the almonds, flour, baking powder and poppy seeds.
- Line an 18 cm/7 in cake tin with baking parchment. Pour the batter into the tin and bake in the oven for 1 hour, or until the cake is golden brown. Turn out the cake on to a rack to cool.

Aunty May's Madeira cake   serves 8

magic ingredient... white flour

The white flour that this cake contains is packed with easy-to-absorb, bone-strengthening calcium, the nutrient that wards against osteoporosis. For its part, the large amount of sugar in the cake gives it a very fine texture.

175 g/6 oz butter, softened
175 g/6 oz caster sugar
3 large eggs, beaten
225 g/8 oz plain white flour, sifted
2 level teaspoons baking powder
2 tablespoons milk
grated zest of 1 lemon
caster sugar to decorate

- Preheat the oven to 160–180°C/325–350°F/gas mark 3–4. Grease and flour a round 18 cm/7 in cake tin.
- Cream the butter with the caster sugar until the mixture is soft and light. Gradually beat in the eggs. Fold in the flour and baking powder, then the milk and lemon zest.
- Spoon the mixture into the cake tin and bake in the oven for 35 to 40 minutes; if the cake is becoming too brown at this point, cover the top with greaseproof paper. If you like a moist cake, test it by inserting a skewer into the centre after a further 40 minutes; if you prefer a slightly drier cake, give it 50 to 55 minutes.
- Allow the cake to cool in the tin for a couple of minutes, then turn it out onto a wire rack and leave it to cool. Decorate with a little caster sugar.

Left: Aunty May's Madeira cake

Date & chocolate cake   serves 8

magic ingredient... chocolate

What more delicious way for your body to receive an iron boost than by eating a slice of this hearty cake, which contains iron-rich chocolate? The fibre in the wholemeal flour slows down the release of sugars into the body, making this a cake that will give you a significant energy boost.

175 g/6 oz unsalted butter
175 g/6 oz light brown sugar
3 medium eggs
2 tablespoons milk
175 g/6 oz wholemeal flour, sifted (reserve husks left in sieve)
2 teaspoons baking powder
225 g/8 oz good-quality plain chocolate, chopped
110 g/4 oz hazelnuts, chopped
50 g/2 oz dates, chopped

- Preheat the oven to 180°C/350°F/gas mark 4. Grease and line a round, loose-bottomed 18 cm/7 in tin.
- Cream the butter and sugar together until the mixture is light and fluffy. Beat the eggs and add to the mixture a little at a time, beating between each addition to avoid curdling.
- Fold the milk, flour (as well as the reserved husks) and baking powder into the mixture, making sure that you combine the ingredients gently, but thoroughly. Add chopped chocolate to the cake mixture with the hazelnuts and dates.
- Pour the mixture into the prepared cake tin and bake for 1¼ to 1½ hours, or until the cake is springy to the touch and a skewer inserted into the middle comes out clean.
- Leave the cake to cool in the tin before removing it and placing it on a wire rack to cool further.

Poppy-seed oatcakes   makes 8

magic ingredient... oats

Oats are rich in 'bad' cholesterol-lowering fibre and contain biotin, a vitamin B complex vitamin that is also known as vitamin H. Biotin can act to prevent hair loss, brittle nails and dermatitis (inflammation of the skin).

75 g/3 oz plain flour
½ teaspoon bicarbonate of soda
75 g/3 oz Demerara sugar
75 g/3 oz porridge oats
75g/3 oz butter
1 tablespoon golden syrup
25 g/1 oz poppy seeds

- Preheat the oven to 170°C/325°F/gas mark 3.
- Sift the flour and bicarbonate of soda into a bowl, add the sugar and oats and mix well.
- In a saucepan, melt the butter and golden syrup over a low heat (do not let the mixture boil) and then pour the liquid over the oat mixture, mixing it in with a wooden spoon.
- When it is cool enough to handle, form the mixture into a ball on a floured surface. Roll it out to a thickness of about 2 cm /¾ in and cut it into rounds.
- Sprinkle the oatcakes with the poppy seeds and place them on a lightly oiled baking sheet. Bake the oatcakes in the oven for 15 minutes, or until they are golden brown. Place them on a wire rack to cool.

Apricot & oat honey muffins   makes 10

magic ingredient... apricots

Apricots contain calcium, a nutrient vital for building strong bones and
preventing osteoporosis. Oatmeal contains lower levels of gluten than
wheat, which makes the muffins easier to digest if you are gluten-sensitive.

150 ml/5 fl oz lukewarm water
½ teaspoon caster sugar
1½ teaspoons dried yeast
150 g/5 oz fine oatmeal
150 g/5 oz cornflour
pinch of salt
125 g/4 oz dried apricots, chopped
1 tablespoon olive oil
3 tablespoons runny honey
Parmesan cheese, freshly grated

- Place half the water in a bowl and add sugar and yeast. Whisk to incorporate as much air as possible. Cover the bowl and leave it in a warm place for 10 minutes.
- Sift the oatmeal, cornflour and salt into another bowl and make a well in the centre. Pour the yeast mixture, dried apricots, olive oil, honey and remaining water into the well. Mix all of the ingredients together to form a dough.
- Knead the dough on a floured surface and then transfer to a bowl. Cover with a clean, damp tea towel and leave in a warm place for about 1 hour, or until risen and double in size.
- Turn out the dough and knead briefly. Divide into 10 pieces and roll into balls. Arrange on a baking tray, sprinkle with flour, cover with a clean tea towel and place in a warm place to rise for a further 45 minutes.
- Preheat the oven to 200°C/400°F/gas mark 6. Grate a little Parmesan cheese over the top of the balls. Bakefor 20 to 25 minutes, or until they are golden brown. (Alternatively, you could cook them in a lightly oiled, heavy-based frying pan for about 5 minutes on each side, until they are brown.)

Ham, Gruyère & crunchy grain-mustard sandwich   makes 1 sandwich

magic ingredient... mustard

Mustard, a great flavour-enhancer, complements the ingredients of this
sandwich perfectly. Ham contains protein, which aids your body to build
strong muscles and furthermore lasts well when lunchtime sandwiches are
made in advance. For their part, tomatoes contain high levels of
potassium, which assists the body to maintain a healthy blood pressure.
Grating the cheese increases its surface area, which heightens its taste,
thus making the sandwich extremely satisfying.

2 slices wholegrain bread, lightly buttered
crunchy grain mustard (quantity optional)
2 slices lean, honey-roast ham
50 g/2 oz Gruyère cheese, grated
crisp green lettuce (quantity optional)
ripe tomatoes (quantity optional)

- Assemble the sandwich by first spreading the bread with a little mustard. Lay the ham and grated cheese on one slice of bread and top with the other. Accompany the sandwich with the lettuce and tomatoes.

sustaining

suppers

The end of the day is the perfect time to sit down and relax over a good meal. Not only can supper be a sociable occasion, but in physiological terms it also enables your body to replenish its nutrient reserves to ensure that you will feel well and full of energy the next morning. The long working hours, family and other pressures that are part and parcel of modern life mean that many people don't have time to have supper until the early hours of the evening – few of us today manage to sit down to eat at 5.30 pm, which was once the usual time for supper. Eating late is not a problem in itself; contrary to popular belief, the body's metabolic rate does not slow down overnight, so you're no more likely to put on weight if you eat later rather than earlier.

The disadvantages of eating late have more to do with other physiological reactions, as well as the way in which the gut is treated. When they finally have time for supper, people who don't eat until late are frequently too hungry to make the best nutritional choices for their bodies. They are far more likely to grab anything that is at all edible from the fridge, reach for some crisps or pick up a kebab or pizza on the way home from work. Even if they manage to hold out until they are in the kitchen, they rarely have the patience and willpower to start chopping up vegetables or to make a sauce from scratch.

There are two main problems associated with eating late and inappropriately. Firstly, if you pick at your food, eat it really quickly, or buy fast food on the way home, the foods that you have chosen will probably not be very healthy, being more than likely to contain high levels of fat and sugar and low levels of beneficial nutrients. Because they are hard for your body to digest, your gut will become irritated if you eat such foods often (especially if you eat a number of them at once and bolt them down quickly) and you will end up feeling as though you have a leaden stomach and/or will suffer from indigestion or bloating. Consuming foods that are difficult to digest late in the evening can furthermore disrupt your sleeping patterns, with the result that you will feel sluggish in the morning. Secondly, your body will be deprived of the opportunity to restock its nutrient reserves. After all, your daily activities will have depleted its store of vitamins and minerals and will have exhausted its glycogen supplies (the major body-fuel reserve that is stored in the liver and muscles), while

moving around will have used up the muscle-bound amino acids (protein 'building blocks'). If you don't replenish these reserves you will expose your body to short-term health problems, such as a weakened immune system, a tendency to catch colds easily and lack of energy, while cancer and heart disease may rear their ugly heads in the future.

Eating well in the evening isn't difficult once you know what your body needs, as well as how rapidly to combine foods that contain beneficial nutrients. Having a snack in the middle of the afternoon or eating a piece of fruit before you leave the office or collect your children from school will help to stave off feelings of hunger until supper, by which time you will still feel strong enough – both physically and mentally – to transform nutritious supper ingredients into a tasty and nourishing meal.

The most relaxing nutrient to eat in the evening is starch, which is contained in bread, rice, polenta, couscous, pasta and potatoes, among other types of food. Such starchy foods encourage your body to produce sleep-inducing hormones – perfect at end of a stressful day – and also play an important part in replenishing your body's glycogen reserves. You should ideally serve vegetables, a salad or fruit (which provide your body with vitamins and minerals) with starchy dishes like my cheesy polenta or pasta with mascarpone cheese, garlic and wild mushrooms (see pages 89 and 91).

Delicious as it is, if you eat pasta every evening you will soon become bored with it and will start to crave different, and not necessarily nutritious, types of food. So make sure that you vary your suppers, alternating starchy meals with such protein-rich dishes as my spicy cod, cabbage leaves stuffed with spicy lamb or lentil casserole (see pages 80, 81 and 84). I have kept the protein sources in all of my supper dishes lean, so you can add extra flavour with a little olive oil or butter if you want without having to worry about your weight. Remember too, that your evening meal doesn't have to be a large one, but could instead be a bowl of my chicken soup with dim sum (see page 79) or carpaccio (see page 83) with a little salad (buy a ready-prepared green, leafy salad and chop some tomatoes into it for a really simple side dish). Alternatively, you could rustle up one of my lunch or breakfast dishes for supper if you fancy it. Even if you're late home from work and don't really feel like eating, the important thing is to eat a little something in the evening – you'll feel much healthier for it the next day.

Lentil, lamb & ginger soup   serves 6

magic ingredient... lentils

The fibre that the lentils contain not only helps to cushion hormonal swings, aid digestion and improve the skin, but also enables the body to produce substances that ward off heart disease and cancer. The ginger in this soup also helps to settle an upset digestive system.

dash of olive oil
1 onion, finely chopped
1 clove garlic, finely chopped
2 teaspoons ground ginger
2 teaspoons garam masala
1.5 litres/2½ pints fresh lamb stock
350 g/12 oz roast lamb meat, shredded
1 carrot, finely chopped
1 small parsnip, finely chopped
1 lemon, cut in half
225 g/8 oz Puy lentils
salt and freshly ground black pepper
250 g/9 oz natural yoghurt

- Heat the olive oil in a large saucepan. Sauté the onion and garlic for about 10 minutes, or until they begin to turn golden brown. Add the ginger and garam masala and stir for 1 minute. Add the stock, lamb, carrot, parsnip, lemon halves and lentils.
- Bring to the boil, cover and then simmer for 25 to 30 minutes, or until the lentils and vegetables are cooked.
- Take the pan off the heat, cool the soup and then remove the lemon. Pour the soup into a blender or liquidiser and blend until smooth.
- Pour the soup into a saucepan, season to taste and gently heat to serving temperature while stirring in the yoghurt, being careful not to boil it as the yoghurt may curdle.

Herb & vegetable soup   serves 4

magic ingredient... vegetables

All of the vegetables in this soup are full of fibre, which enables the digestive system to work efficiently by encouraging the bowel to excrete waste products regularly, thereby helping to avoid constipation.

225 g/8 oz uncooked, brown rice (with husks intact)
3 tablespoons olive oil
½ teaspoon salt
2 large onions, finely chopped
2 cloves garlic, finely chopped
2 stalks celery, finely sliced
2 medium-sized carrots, sliced
1.5 litres/2½ pints vegetable stock
12 ripe plum tomatoes
1 head endive, chopped
4 tablespoons fresh parsley, chopped
2 tablespoons fresh basil, torn into fine strips
salt and freshly ground black pepper
Parmesan cheese, freshly grated (optional)

- Gently sauté the rice in 1 tablespoon of olive oil for a couple of minutes to separate the grains. Then add twice as much cold water as rice to the pan, along with the salt. Bring to the boil and simmer for about 25 minutes, or until the rice is cooked – it should be nutty, but not mushy.
- Meanwhile, gently sauté the onions, garlic, celery and carrots in 2 tablespoons of olive oil for about 10 minutes, or until they are soft and golden brown in colour. Add the stock, tomatoes and endive. Simmer for 10 minutes. Stir in the rice, parsley and basil.
- Before serving, season to taste and sprinkle with a little freshly grated Parmesan cheese.

Mint soup   serves 4

magic ingredient... mint

While soup is generally easy to digest, mint further soothes an upset
stomach, making this a comforting and settling dish if you are suffering
from digestive problems.

1 large onion, finely chopped
3 tablespoons olive oil
4 tomatoes, peeled and chopped
1 green pepper, finely chopped
3 tablespoons fresh mint, finely chopped
1 litre/35 fl oz chicken or vegetable stock
salt and freshly ground black pepper
4 large cloves garlic, chopped

- In a saucepan, coat the onion in the olive oil over a low heat. Add the tomatoes, pepper and 2 tablespoons of mint. Add the stock to the vegetables and season with salt and pepper. Add the garlic, bring to the boil, cover and simmer for 20 minutes.
- Stir in the rest of the mint and serve immediately. If you would like to serve this soup cold in summer, adapt the recipe as follows. Omit the olive oil. Place all of the ingredients apart from 1 tablespoon of fresh mint in a saucepan and simmer for 20 minutes. Leave the soup to cool and then chill it in the fridge. Serve poured over ice cubes and garnish with the remaining chopped mint.

Pasta, lentil & tomato soup   serves 6

magic ingredient... pasta

Pasta is a comforting and settling food, and encourages the body to
produce relaxing hormones, making it ideal for an evening meal.

3 tablespoons olive oil
2 onions, finely chopped
6 cloves garlic, finely chopped
2 sticks celery, finely chopped
110 g/4 oz smoked streaky bacon, chopped into small pieces
225 g/8 oz Puy lentils
4 tomatoes, skinned, de-seeded and chopped
400 g/14 oz tin chopped plum tomatoes
2 bay leaves
3–4 sprigs fresh thyme
1.5 litres/2½ pints chicken stock, plus a further 275 ml/½ pint
225 g/8 oz macaroni or similar small pasta shapes
salt and freshly ground black pepper
2–3 tablespoons fresh parsley, chopped
75–110 g/3–4 oz Parmesan cheese, freshly grated

- Heat the oil in a large, heavy-bottomed casserole, add the onions, garlic, celery and bacon and cook over a low heat for about 10 to 15 minutes, or until the vegetables are soft and translucent.
- Add the lentils and stir well to ensure that they are coated in oil. Add the fresh and tinned tomatoes, bring to the boil, and then add the bay leaves, thyme and 1.5 litres/2½ pints of the stock. Simmer for about 40 minutes, or until the lentils are cooked. If the mixture is absorbing a lot of stock, add some more, keeping the level above the lentils.
- Cook the macaroni in boiling water, drain well and add to the soup, along with an extra couple of ladles of stock. Season well and garnish with parsley.
- Serve the soup in bowls, sprinkled with Parmesan cheese.

Chicken soup with dim sum   serves 4

magic ingredient... chicken

Chicken is full of lean protein, which is vital for building strong muscles and repairing body cells when broken down by the body into amino acids. It is best to buy organic, free-range chicken to ensure that it doesn't contain antibiotics and other drugs.

Dim sum filling
2 cloves garlic, finely chopped
1 teaspoon grated fresh ginger
1 teaspoon each plum sauce, light soy sauce and Thai fish sauce
pinch of chilli powder
pinch of five-spice powder
1 bunch spring onions, chopped
1 egg white
200 g/7 oz cooked chicken breast, skin removed and finely chopped
75 g/3 oz cooked prawns, finely chopped

Wrapper dough
275 g/9 oz plain flour, plus a little extra for kneading
250 ml/8 fl oz boiling water

Chicken soup
750 ml/1½ pint chicken stock
1–2 teaspoons light soy sauce
1 teaspoon rice wine
1 teaspoon sesame oil
25 g/1 oz bean sprouts
2 large leaves pak choi, shredded
1 carrot, cut into fine strips
8 fresh shiitake mushrooms, sliced

- First make the dim sum filling by mixing the garlic, ginger, plum sauce, soy sauce, fish sauce, chilli powder, five-spice powder, spring onions and the egg white together in a bowl. Stir in the chopped chicken and prawns. Cover and leave to marinate in the fridge for 1 to 2 hours.
- To make the wrapper dough, first place the flour in a large bowl and make a well in the centre. Slowly pour the boiling water into the well, mixing it in with a knife. Continue mixing until all of the water has been absorbed (if the mixture appears wet, add a little extra flour). Leave to stand for about 3 minutes, or until it is cool enough to handle.
- With your fingers, gather together the dough to form a ball (it should be soft and pliable). Knead the dough on a lightly floured work surface for about 5 minutes, or until it is smooth and elastic. Cover the dough with a clean tea towel and leave it at room temperature for 30 minutes.
- To make the soup, first put the chicken stock into a saucepan with 1 teaspoon of the soy sauce and the rice wine and bring to the boil. Heat the sesame oil in a wok or non-stick frying pan and stir-fry the vegetables, adding a splash or two of water to prevent the vegetables from sticking to the pan. Add the vegetables to the soup and boil for 2 minutes. Taste the soup and add a little more soy sauce if you like.
- Cut the wrapper dough in half and roll out each half into a cylinder. Cut each cylinder into 12 slices. Lightly flour a work surface and, using a rolling pin, roll and flatten each slice into a circle about 10 cm/4 in in diameter.
- Divide the dim sum filling between the 24 wrappers, lightly moisten the edge of each wrapper with water (take care not to use too much) and fold it over to form a semi-circle; press down the edge to seal the dim sum. Cover the dim sum with a clean, damp tea towel to prevent them from drying out until you are ready to cook them.
- To serve, steam the dim sum in a bamboo steamer over a saucepan of boiling water for 8 to 10 minutes or sauté them in a wok for about 4 minutes, or until they are golden. Ladle the soup and vegetables into 4 soup bowls. Add 6 dim sum to each bowl and serve.

Left: Chicken soup with dim sum

Roasted red mullet   serves 4

magic ingredient... red mullet

Red mullet contains lean protein, as well as the beneficial fish oils omega-3 and omega-6 fatty acids, both of which protect against heart disease.

1 red mullet with livers intact, 1.5 kg/3 lb, gutted, washed and
  patted dry
5 tablespoons cold water
½ tablespoon salt
2 cloves garlic, peeled and finely chopped
1 fresh bay leaf
1 sprig rosemary, leaves removed
2 tablespoons olive oil

- First, grill the red mullet. Ideally, you should cook the fish on a barbecue, over an even and quite gentle heat. If you are unable to use a barbecue, however, grill the fish under a preheated medium grill for about 6 minutes on each side, depending on the thickness of the fish.
- Meanwhile, prepare the dressing. Mix the water and salt together in a small pan. Crush the chopped garlic and stir it into the salt water. Add the bay leaf, rosemary and olive oil and stir carefully. Using the back of a spoon, press the rosemary and bay leaf hard to encourage them to release their flavours into the water. Over a low heat, warm the dressing through until it is just tepid.
- Once the fish is cooked, carefully transfer it to a warmed serving plate and pour the dressing over it. Serve at once.

Spicy cod   serves 4

magic ingredient... olive oil

Olive oil is a vegetable oil that encourages the body to increase its production of high-density lipoprotein (HDL), the 'good' cholesterol that helps to ward off heart disease, as well as generating energy and metabolising the fat-soluble vitamins A, D, E and K.

450 g/1 lb cod fillets, trimmed, washed and patted dry
1 onion, peeled and finely sliced
3 cloves garlic, peeled and crushed
450 g/1 lb vine-ripened tomatoes
2 tablespoons tomato purée
10 black olives, pitted
2 handfuls fresh, curly-leaved parsley, chopped
1 tablespoon olive oil
salt and freshly ground black pepper
2 tablespoons capers, drained and finely chopped
4 sardines (tinned in oil), roughly chopped
1 potato, peeled and grated
4 tablespoons fresh fish stock
5 cm/2 in-long dried red chilli pepper
juice of 1 lime, strained

- Place the cod in a heavy-bottomed saucepan and cover it with the onion, garlic, tomatoes, tomato purée, olives, parsley and olive oil. Season with salt and pepper and cook gently over a low heat for about 10 minutes. Remove the cod and vegetables from the saucepan, arrange them on a warmed serving plate and keep them hot in a preheated oven.
- Add the capers to the remaining oil in the saucepan and stir. Add the sardines to the capers. Stir in the potato, stock and chilli. Stir and simmer for about 5 minutes, or until the potato is cooked through.
- Remove the chilli from the sauce and the serving plate from the oven. Pour the sauce over the cod and vegetables and sprinkle with the lime juice before serving.

Cabbage leaves stuffed with spicy lamb   serves 4

magic ingredient... lamb

Lamb is usually a low-allergenic and easily digestible food. Using it within a stuffing, as in this dish, is an excellent way to encourage children to eat meat, which is a good source of protein.

1 Savoy cabbage
1 large onion, finely chopped
2 cloves garlic, finely chopped
dash of olive oil
225 g/8 oz red lentils, cooked
1 tablespoon raisins or sultanas
1 large tomato, finely chopped
1 teaspoon ground cinnamon
½ teaspoon ground allspice
2 tablespoons basil, finely torn
salt and freshly ground black pepper
225 g/8 oz cold cooked lamb, minced or finely chopped
2 tablespoons fresh mint, chopped
1 tablespoon tamarind paste soaked in 2 tablespoons water
  and mixed with ½ teaspoon sugar

- Preheat the oven to 200°C/400°F/gas mark 6.
- Separate the cabbage leaves and remove the thick part of the stalk from each leaf. Cook the leaves in a large pan, just covered with boiling water, for 1 to 2 minutes. Drain well.
- Sauté the onion and garlic in a dash of olive oil until they are transparent. Add the lentils, raisins or sultanas, tomato, cinnamon, allspice and basil and season to taste. Stir well and turn off the heat. Add the lamb and 1 tablespoon of the chopped mint and mix thoroughly.
- Place 1 heaped tablespoon of the lamb mixture in the centre of each leaf. Fold two sides of the leaf over the filling and then roll up to enclose the filling completely (secure with cocktail sticks).
- Grease a casserole dish with a little olive oil, line the dish with any unfilled cabbage leaves and arrange the filled ones on top. Pour the tamarind juice over the cabbage pouches, cover with foil and bake in the oven for 20 minutes. Remove the foil, sprinkle the pouches with the remaining mint and serve.

Chicken livers with mint & yoghurt   serves 2

magic ingredient... yoghurt

Yoghurt provides the body with calcium, an important nutrient for the maintenance of bones. It is vital that menopausal women and children in particular, eat food that contains plenty of calcium, the former in order to guard against osteoporosis and the latter to build strong bones.

300 g/11 oz chicken livers
2 medium-sized onions, finely chopped
1 clove garlic, finely chopped
2 tablespoons olive oil
2 heaped tablespoons plain white flour
salt and freshly ground black pepper
6 tablespoons thick, natural yoghurt
1 tablespoon fresh mint, finely chopped

- Clean the chicken livers thoroughly, removing any black or green bits.
- Sauté the onions and garlic in a little of the olive oil, until they are soft and slightly golden brown in colour.
- Mix the flour with some salt and freshly ground black pepper and spread over a plate. Toss the chicken livers in the seasoned flour to coat them lightly.
- Using a slotted spoon, remove the onions and garlic from the pan and put to one side. Sauté the chicken livers in the rest of the olive oil until they are golden brown. Add the onion and garlic and cook until the ingredients are piping hot.
- Remove the pan from the heat and add the yoghurt. Stir well and season to taste. Sprinkle with fresh mint and serve.

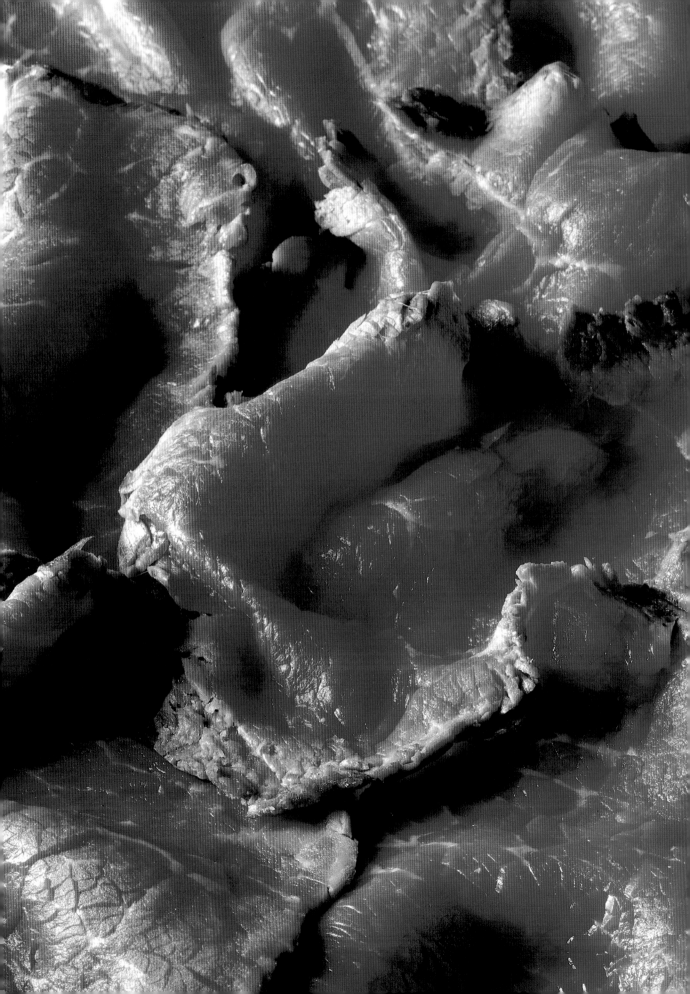

Carpaccio   serves 6

magic ingredient... lean red beef

The lean red beef in this carpaccio is rich in zinc, which strengthens the
immune system, and contains high levels of easily absorbed iron, making it
an anaemia-hindering food. This dish should be made the day before you
are planning to serve it. You may have to order the beef from your
butcher in advance.

Marinade
5 tablespoons olive oil
juice of 1 lemon
small handful each fresh thyme and rosemary, stalks removed
salt and freshly ground black pepper

Beef and garnish
450 g/1 lb well-hung fillet of beef
dash of olive oil
salt and freshly ground black pepper
2 small chillies, de-seeded and sliced into very thin pieces
15 g/½ oz fresh coriander leaves, chopped
2 cloves garlic, crushed
juice of 1 lemon
shavings of Parmesan cheese

- Mix together the ingredients for the marinade in a small bowl.
  Place the beef in a non-metallic dish, pour the marinade over it
  and cover. Leave to marinate overnight in the fridge.
- Drain the marinade from the beef. Heat a dash of olive oil in a
  heavy-bottomed frying pan until it begins to smoke. Place the
  beef in the oil and turn it over several times to brown it all over
  and seal in the flavours. Remove the beef from the heat, place
  it on a plate and leave it in the fridge for at least 2 hours.
- Using a very sharp carving knife, slice the beef as thinly as you
  can. Place each slice between two sheets of baking paper and
  thin it out with a rolling pin until it is almost transparent. Gently
  lift the slices of beef off the paper and arrange them on plates,
  allowing 3 to 4 slices per person.
- Serve sprinkled with a dash of olive oil, salt and pepper, chillies,
  coriander leaves, garlic and lemon juice. Finally, sprinkle a little
  shaved Parmesan cheese over the top.

Prawn & Emmental salad   serves 4

magic ingredient... prawns

Prawns are rich in the libido-boosting nutrient zinc. As well as adversely
affecting the sex drive, a lack of zinc in the body can lead to sterility and
birth defects. This easy-to-make dish incorporates many colours, textures,
smells and tastes, making it extremely organoleptic.

1 curly-leaved lettuce
salt and freshly ground black pepper
2 tablespoons white wine vinegar
150 ml/5 fl oz olive oil
24 large raw prawns, shells attached
200 g/7 oz Emmental cheese, diced
1 small courgette, sliced
1 green apple, unpeeled and diced

- Wash and tear the lettuce leaves. Make the dressing by mixing
  together the salt, pepper, vinegar and oil.
- Place the prawns in a pan of simmering, salted water, bring to
  the boil, cook for 3 minutes and then plunge them into cold
  water. Drain and shell the prawns.
- Arrange the lettuce leaves, prawns, Emmental cubes, courgette
  slices and diced apple on a plate. Sprinkle with the dressing and
  serve.

Left: Carpaccio

Lentil casserole   serves 4

magic ingredient... lentils

A high-fibre food, lentils help to keep the gut healthy, aid digestion and
also reduce the risk of developing heart disease and cancer. To add
variety, you could serve this dish with lean sausages, fish (such as fresh
tuna or mackerel fillets) or grilled vegetables.

1 tablespoon olive oil
1 red onion, finely chopped
3 cloves garlic, finely chopped
1 large carrot, grated
225 g/8 oz green or brown lentils
400 g/14 oz tin plum tomatoes
110 g/4 oz sultanas (optional)
1 teaspoon garam masala
1 teaspoon cumin seeds
1 teaspoon fennel seeds
1 teaspoon coriander seeds, crushed
salt and freshly ground black pepper
2 tablespoons fresh herbs, such as basil or coriander, chopped

- Heat the oil in a large pan. Add the onion, garlic and carrot and
  sauté for 10 minutes. Add the lentils and sauté for 3 minutes.
  Stir in the tomatoes and, if you are using them, sultanas, and
  enough water to cover the lentils. Boil rapidly for 10 minutes
  and then simmer for 20 to 30 minutes, or until the lentils are
  soft. Stir occasionally, adding more water if necessary.
- Stir in the garam masala, cumin seeds, fennel seeds, coriander
  seeds and salt and pepper to taste. Simmer for 5 minutes to
  allow the lentils to absorb the flavours of the herbs and spices.
- Just before serving, add 2 tablespoons of chopped fresh herbs.

Caponata   serves 4

magic ingredient... garlic

Eating plenty of garlic will reduce the risk that you will develop a blood
clot or thrombosis, because garlic contains substances that prevent blood
vessels from becoming blocked by blood cells.

4 aubergines
salt and freshly ground black pepper
4 tablespoons olive oil
2 shallots, finely chopped
2 cloves garlic, finely chopped
8 plum tomatoes, skins removed, de-seeded and roughly
  chopped
4 sticks celery, finely chopped
2 tablespoons capers, rinsed
50 g/2 oz black olives, pitted
4 tablespoons red wine vinegar
1 tablespoon dark brown sugar
5 tablespoons flat-leaved parsley, chopped
1 tablespoon basil, torn

- Cut the aubergines into 2.5 cm/1 in cubes. Sprinkle the cubes
  with salt and leave for 45 minutes.
- Rinse the aubergine cubes under cold running water and dry
  them with a kitchen towel or clean tea towel.
- Heat the olive oil in a frying pan and add the aubergine cubes.
  Cook them for about 10 minutes, or until soft and golden
  brown (you may need to do this in two batches). Remove them
  from the pan and place them on sheets of kitchen towel to
  drain away any excess fat.
- Sauté the shallots and garlic until soft and turning golden
  brown. Add the tomatoes and celery and cook gently for 20
  minutes. Add the capers, olives, vinegar and sugar and season
  to taste. Cook gently for a further 20 minutes and then add the
  aubergine cubes. Mix all of the ingredients together and reheat
  thoroughly.
- Before serving, sprinkle the herbs over the top of the dish.

Aubergine stir-fry serves 4

magic ingredient... garlic

Garlic helps to prevent 'bad' cholesterol or low-density lipoprotein (LDL), from being deposited in the blood vessels by raising the level of high-density lipoprotein (HDL) in the blood. HDL sweeps up excess LDL and carries it to the bowel, where it is excreted.

2 medium-sized aubergines
1 teaspoon salt
2 tablespoons fresh thyme leaves
4 tablespoons sesame oil
300 g/11 oz lean lamb fillet
8 cloves garlic, peeled and finely chopped
6 spring onions, sliced
6 vine-ripened tomatoes, chopped
225 g/8 oz bag of spinach, stalks and stems removed and
  finely chopped
salt and freshly ground black pepper

- Cut the aubergines into 2.5 cm/1 in cubes and place in a small bowl with the salt, thyme and 2 tablespoons of the sesame oil. Allow the aubergine cubes to marinate for 30 minutes.
- Slice the lamb into thin strips. Heat a wok over a high heat. Add the remaining sesame oil and when the oil starts to crackle, add the aubergine cubes and fry until soft and light golden brown. Remove from the wok using a slotted spoon and place on kitchen paper to drain off the excess oil.
- Return the wok to the heat. When the oil starts to crackle again, add the garlic, onions and lamb and cook for a couple of minutes, stirring constantly, until the lamb changes colour. Add the tomatoes and cook until they have started to soften.
- Just before serving, add the aubergines and spinach to the wok and toss the ingredients for 30 seconds or so, until they are sizzling hot. Season with salt and pepper and serve at once.

Tomato & buffalo mozzarella lasagne serves 6

magic ingredient... mozzarella

Buffalo mozzarella is rich in calcium, which is essential for the formation and maintenance of strong teeth and bones. This is therefore an excellent dish to give to children, whose bones are still growing and hardening.

25 g/1 oz butter or a dash of olive oil
2 onions, thinly sliced
2 carrots, thinly sliced
1 clove garlic, crushed (optional)
1.8 kg/4 1b tomatoes, skinned, de-seeded and chopped
4 tablespoons fresh basil, torn
2 teaspoons sugar (optional)
salt and freshly ground black pepper
8 fresh lasagne pasta sheets
225 g/8 oz spinach, stems removed and washed
200 g/7 oz buffalo mozzarella, sliced
freshly grated nutmeg
Parmesan cheese, freshly grated
1 large bunch fresh basil, torn

- Melt the butter or heat the olive oil in a saucepan. Add the onions and carrots (and garlic if you are using it) and cook until the vegetables have softened.
- Add the tomatoes, basil and sugar and season to taste. Allow the tomato sauce to simmer for 15 minutes.
- Preheat the oven to 190°C/375°F/gas mark 5.
- In an ovenproof dish, build up layers of lasagne, spinach, tomato sauce and mozzarella (when adding the spinach, grate a little nutmeg over it to enhance its taste). Finish with a layer of mozzarella, season and grate some fresh Parmesan cheese over the top.
- Bake in the oven for 40 minutes, or until the lasagne is bubbling and hot. Serve with the torn basil scattered over the top.

Stuffed field mushrooms   serves 4

magic ingredient... tahini

The sesame seeds in the tahini provide the body with a useful non-dairy source of calcium, the nutrient that plays a vital role in strengthening bones and teeth. It is safer to buy field mushrooms rather than gathering them yourself, in case you inadvertently harvest poisonous ones.

2 aubergines
dash of olive oil
8 large field mushrooms
1 clove garlic, finely chopped
2 teaspoons fresh thyme, chopped
2 teaspoon tahini (sesame-seed paste)
4 tablespoons Greek-style yoghurt
juice of 1 lemon
75 g/3 oz lean bacon, cooked and finely chopped
salt and freshly ground black pepper

- Preheat the oven to 200°C/400°F/gas mark 6.
- Wash the aubergines, prick them all over with a fork (to allow steam to escape while roasting) and brush with a little olive oil. Place on a baking tray and roast for 40 minutes until soft.
- Cut the stalks off the mushrooms and arrange with undersides upwards on a baking tray. Drizzle a little olive oil over the top and bake for 5 minutes. Remove the mushrooms from the oven and allow them to cool.
- When cool enough to handle, cut the aubergines in half and scoop out the flesh. Mash the flesh with a fork (or use a hand-held blender) and add the garlic, thyme, tahini, yoghurt and lemon juice, stirring well until the purée is smooth. Add bacon and season. Heap the purée onto the mushrooms and serve.

Asparagus, fennel & walnut salad   serves 4

magic ingredient... fennel

The fennel in this salad is excellent for soothing a disturbed digestive system, providing as it does a subtle flavour without further irritating an unsettled gut. Fennel is also a mild diuretic.

Dressing
2 medium-sized potatoes, peeled, diced and cooked
finely grated zest and juice of 2 oranges
2 tablespoons fromage frais
1 tablespoon low fat yoghurt
2 tablespoons walnut oil
salt and freshly ground black pepper

Salad
1 bunch asparagus, trimmed and cut into 3 cm/1 in pieces
2 fennel bulbs, thinly sliced
1 curly endive (frisée)
6 walnuts, roasted and chopped into quarters
6 tablespoons mixed herbs (parsley, chervil, coriander) chopped
juice of 1 orange

- Make the dressing by placing the potatoes, orange zest and juice, fromage frais, yoghurt and walnut oil in a food processor. Blend until smooth and season to taste with salt and pepper.
- Steam the asparagus for 2 minutes, refresh in ice-cold water, then drain well. Steam the fennel for 2 minutes and set aside.
- Tear the heart of the curly endive into small pieces and mix the leaves with the walnuts and herbs. Toss the salad in the orange juice.
- Arrange the salad in the centre of a serving dish and pile the steamed asparagus and fennel on top. Spoon some of the dressing over the salad and coarsely grind some black pepper over it. Serve the remaining dressing separately.

Left: Stuffed field mushrooms

Chicken & mushroom savoury crumble   serves 6

magic ingredient... wholemeal flour

Wholemeal flour contains high levels of fibre, which increases the satiety
or 'fullness' qualities of the dish – that is, you will feel comfortably full
without having eaten a large amount. This crumble is delicious served with
such green leafy vegetables as spinach, Savoy cabbage or broccoli spears.

175 g/6 oz butter
225 g/8 oz wholemeal flour
175 g/6 oz oat flakes
pinch of salt
25 g/1 oz unsalted butter
2 onions, finely chopped
2 sticks celery, scrubbed and finely chopped
1 chicken, weighing approximately 1.6 kg/3½ lb, complete
   with innards
1 teaspoon salt
freshly ground black pepper
2 bay leaves
450 g/1 lb flat field mushrooms, trimmed and thinly sliced
Worcestershire sauce
1 level tablespoon plain flour
75 ml/2½ fl oz double cream
1 tablespoon fresh parsley, chopped

- Make the crumble topping by rubbing 175 g/6 oz butter into
  the flour using the tips of your fingers, until the mixture
  resembles breadcrumbs. Add the oat flakes and salt and mix
  lightly, again using only your fingertips (otherwise the heat
  from your hands will melt the butter and turn it into pastry).
  Place the mixture in the fridge.
- Melt 14 g/½ oz of the unsalted butter in a large, heavy-based
  pan over a low heat and cook the onions and celery for about
  10 minutes, until they are soft and just beginning to colour.
- Remove the liver and giblets from the chicken and wash and
  wipe the chicken, inside and out. Wash the giblets and liver.
  Place the chicken, giblets and liver in the pan with the onion
  and celery and pour over enough water to cover the chicken.
  Bring to the boil, remove any scum and add 1 teaspoon of salt,
  freshly ground black pepper and 1 bay leaf.
- Cover the pan with a lid and simmer gently for about 1½ hours,
  or until the chicken is tender. Lift the chicken out of the pan,
  place it on a warm dish and keep it hot. Strain the cooking
  liquid and set it aside.
- Preheat the oven to 200°C/400°F/gas mark 6.
- Melt the remaining butter in a small pan and cook the
  mushrooms over a low heat for 2 to 3 minutes. Add a few
  drops of Worcestershire sauce and sprinkle the flour over the
  mushrooms. Cook, stirring continuously, until all of the fat has
  been absorbed into the flour. Gradually blend in about 150
  ml/¼ pint of the strained chicken liquid to make a smooth
  sauce. Adjust the seasoning if necessary. Stir in the cream and
  heat the sauce through (but do not let it boil).
- Carve the chicken and arrange the slices and joints in a deep
  casserole dish. Pour the mushroom sauce over the top and
  garnish with chopped parsley. Tear up the remaining bay leaf
  and sprinkle it over the top. Top with the crumble mixture and
  place the dish in the oven for 20 minutes, or until the crumble
  topping has turned golden brown.

Chicken & pumpkin curry serves 4–6

magic ingredient... garlic

Garlic contains high levels of allicin, a powerful nutrient that can help to prevent heart disease. It also plays a helpful role in reducing high blood pressure, as well as enhancing the flavour of dishes such as this.

450 g/1 lb pumpkin or squash, peeled and cut into small cubes
dash of olive oil
1 medium-sized onion, finely chopped
6 cloves garlic, finely chopped
1 teaspoon turmeric
1 teaspoon ground cumin
1 green chilli, de-seeded and finely chopped
3 cloves
1 teaspoon fresh root ginger, finely chopped
1.8 kg/4 1b raw chicken breasts, chopped into bite-sized
  pieces
250 ml/8 fl oz coconut milk
salt and freshly ground black pepper
2 tablespoons fresh coriander, chopped

- Steam the pumpkin or squash cubes for 5 minutes, or boil for 10 minutes, until tender. Drain and put to one side.
- Heat the olive oil in a large saucepan and sauté the onion and garlic for a few minutes, or until they have become translucent. Add the turmeric, cumin and chilli and cook for 1 minute to warm them through. Add the cloves, ginger and chicken. Simmer for 8 minutes, stirring from time to time.
- Add the pumpkin or squash cubes and stir well. Simmer for 20 minutes, watching carefully and stirring occasionally to ensure that the curry doesn't burn.
- Pour the coconut milk into the pan and bring the sauce slowly to simmering point, stirring all the time. Season to taste and garnish with fresh coriander before serving.

Cheesy polenta serves 6

magic ingredient... polenta

As well as being gluten-free, polenta is a carbohydrate-rich food that stimulates the production of relaxing, sleep-inducing hormones. Although polenta can be served as an accompaniment to roast meats, fish and vegetables, I love to make it with cheese as a simple comfort dish. It is also rather delicious when it has been allowed to become cold and is then grilled and served with a rich tomato sauce.

225 g/8 oz polenta
1 tablespoon salt
1.3 litres/2¼ pints cold water, milk or a mixture of both
freshly ground black pepper
75 g/3 oz unsalted butter
50 g/2 oz Parmesan cheese, freshly grated

- Pour the polenta into a heavy-bottomed, non-stick saucepan with a capacity of 2.4 litres /4 pints. Mix in the salt and gradually add the water or milk, stirring constantly with a wooden spoon to ensure that there are no lumps.
- Place the pan over a medium-high heat and stir constantly for about 5 minutes, or until the polenta starts to thicken. Turn down the heat and simmer for 20 minutes, stirring regularly, until the polenta pulls away from the sides of the pan. Season with lots of freshly ground black pepper.
- Pour the mixture into a bowl and make a well in the centre. Put the butter into the well, sprinkle with Parmesan cheese, mix well and serve at once.

Vegetable couscous serves 6

magic ingredient...

Carrots contain high levels of the antioxidant betacarotene, which assists the immune system to build up its defences against disease. Harissa, a hot, red-pimento Tunisian paste, can now be found in most supermarkets. It should be liberally diluted in the sauce, the sauce itself being poured over the couscous in small amounts. Yoghurt and a tomato salad make good accompaniments to this nutritious dish.

2 onions, chopped
2 cloves garlic, finely chopped
225 g/8 oz carrots, sliced
225 g/8 oz pumpkin, squash or turnip, cut into chunks
2 tablespoons olive oil
½ teaspoon fresh root ginger, grated
salt and freshly ground black pepper
175 g/6 oz peas and/or cooked chickpeas
1 aubergine, cut into cubes
3 courgettes, sliced
50 g/2 oz broad beans
100 g/3½ oz sultanas or raisins
3 tomatoes, chopped
½ teaspoon chilli powder
2 teaspoons paprika
15 g/½ oz fresh coriander or parsley, stalks removed and
  chopped (retain the leaves for garnish)
450 g/1 lb couscous
225 g/8 oz bag of spinach, finely shredded
1–2 teaspoons harissa paste

- Sauté the onions, garlic, carrots and pumpkin, squash or turnip in the olive oil in a large saucepan for 5 minutes. Pour over enough water to cover the vegetables, add the ginger, season with salt and pepper and simmer for 20 minutes.
- Add the peas and/or chickpeas, aubergine, courgettes, broad beans, sultanas or raisins, tomatoes, chilli powder, paprika, coriander or parsley stalks and stir well. Pour over enough extra water to cover the vegetables.
- Place the couscous in a sieve and rest it across the top of the saucepan. Cover the sieve with a lid and steam for 30 minutes or so, while the vegetables cook underneath. (Many varieties of couscous are pre-cooked, so follow the packet instructions. If you prefer to cook the couscous in a separate pan, partially cook it and then transfer it to a sieve and place it over the saucepan containing the vegetables for 10 minutes so that it can absorb the flavours of the vegetables from the steam.)
- To make the sauce, first remove 6 tablespoons of the vegetable liquid and transfer it to a warmed bowl. Add the spinach and stir well. Stir in the harissa paste and mix well.
- When you are ready to serve the dish, pile the couscous into a bowl and make a well in the centre. Fill the well with the vegetable mixture and sprinkle the reserved parsley or coriander leaves over the top. Serve the sauce separately.

Pasta with mascarpone cheese, garlic & wild mushrooms   serves 2–4

magic ingredient... pasta

Because pasta encourages the body to produce relaxing hormones, it
makes a great food to unwind over in the evening after a long and
stressful day. The herbs and vegetables provide plenty of flavour.

25 g/1 oz dried wild mushrooms
225 g/8 oz fresh mushrooms
200 g/7 oz dried pasta shapes
2 tablespoons olive oil
½ a small onion, chopped
2 cloves garlic, finely chopped
2 sprigs thyme
1 bay leaf
4 tablespoons mascarpone cheese
2 teaspoons fresh parsley, chopped
2 teaspoons fresh marjoram, chopped
salt and freshly ground black pepper

- Cover the dried mushrooms with 85 ml/3 fl oz boiling water
  and leave to soak until softened. Stir them around to clean
  thoroughly. Remove from the water (reserve the liquid) and pat
  dry with a kitchen towel. Strain the liquid through a coffee filter
  and set it aside. Slice the mushrooms thinly.
- Clean the fresh mushrooms and remove any tough parts from
  their stems. Slice the mushrooms thinly.
- Put the pasta on to boil in salted water to which 1 teaspoon of
  olive oil has been added and cook until the pasta is *al dente*.
- In another pan, heat the olive oil and gently sauté the onion
  and garlic until the onion is light golden brown. Add the dried
  and fresh mushrooms, the thyme, bay leaf and mascarpone
  cheese and bring slowly to the boil. Pour in the strained
  mushroom liquid, add the parsley, marjoram, salt and pepper
  and cook gently for 5 minutes.
- Drain the cooked pasta. Add the sauce to the pasta and stir
  well. Grate some black pepper over the top and serve at once.

Tomato, goats' cheese & broad bean risotto   serves 2

magic ingredient... rice

The rice in this wheat-free, carbohydrate-rich recipe helps to induce
feelings of sleepiness, making it a delicious and sustaining dish to enjoy in
the evening in anticipation of a good night's sleep.

1 tablespoon olive oil
50 g/2 oz shallots, finely chopped
1 clove garlic, finely chopped
350 g/12 oz risotto rice
1.5 litres/2½ pints fresh chicken or vegetable stock, warmed
100 ml/4 fl oz dry white wine
25 g/1 oz butter
175 g/6 oz frozen broad beans, defrosted
110 g/4 oz creamy goats' cheese, crumbled
110 g/4 oz sun-dried tomatoes
50 g/2 oz Parmesan cheese, freshly grated
salt and freshly ground black pepper

- Place the olive oil in a large saucepan and warm it over a gentle
  heat. Add the shallots and garlic. Cook for 2 to 3 minutes, or
  until the shallots have softened and have started to become
  clear. Add the risotto rice and stir well to heat all of the grains.
- Bring the stock to boil in another saucepan and then gradually
  add it to the rice, a cup at a time, stirring well until the rice has
  absorbed each cupful and is tender, but still *al dente* (it
  shouldn't be mushy). Pour in the wine.
- Turn off the heat and add the butter, broad beans, goats'
  cheese, tomatoes and Parmesan cheese. Season to taste, using
  lots of freshly ground black pepper. Serve at once.

Strawberries with balsamic vinegar   serves 6–8

magic ingredient... strawberries

Strawberries are packed with vitamin C, a powerful tissue-repairing
nutrient that can also help to clear up spotty skin. Balsamic vinegar and
strawberries is an unusual but delectable combination.

1.5 kg/3 lb strawberries, hulled and cut in half lengthwise
50 g/2 oz icing sugar
3 tablespoons balsamic vinegar

- Place the strawberries in a large serving bowl. Sprinkle the icing sugar over the strawberries and pour the vinegar over the top. Toss well and chill for at least 1 hour. Toss again lightly just before serving.

Berries with mascarpone cheese   serves 6

magic ingredient... mascarpone

The mascarpone cheese in this dish is rich in vitamin D, a nutrient that
plays an essential role in assisting calcium to build and maintain strong
bones and teeth. Vitamin D in the body is mainly generated by sunlight,
so this dessert will help to top up your intake of this vitamin if you
haven't been able to go outside for some time.

450 g/1 lb raspberries
225 g/8 oz blueberries
900 g/2 lb strawberries, hulled and cut in half lengthwise
225 g/8 oz mascarpone cheese
170 ml/6 fl oz natural yoghurt
75 g/3 oz icing sugar

- Set half of the raspberries to one side. Combine the remaining raspberries, blueberries and strawberries in a large mixing bowl. Mix the mascarpone cheese and yoghurt in a small mixing bowl until smooth.
- In a blender, purée the reserved raspberries with the icing sugar until the raspberries are smooth and the icing sugar has completely dissolved.
- To serve, place a little raspberry sauce on to each plate and arrange a pile of berries in the centre. Top with a dollop of the mascarpone mixture.

Left: Strawberries with balsamic vinegar

Raspberry & ginger cheesecake   serves 4

magic ingredient... raspberries

Raspberries contain high levels of vitamin C, the antioxidant vitamin that
helps the body to absorb iron, as well as aiding the healing of wounds,
promoting growth and protecting against colds.

Base
225 g/8 oz good-quality stem-ginger biscuits
50 g/2 oz unsalted butter

Topping
50 ml/2 fl oz double cream
50 ml/2 fl oz thick fromage frais
125 g/4½ oz mascarpone cheese
2 tablespoons caster sugar
560 g/1 lb 4 oz fresh raspberries
2 tablespoons acacia or runny honey
juice of 1 unwaxed lemon

- To make the base, first crush the ginger biscuits. Melt the
  butter in a small pan and then add the crushed biscuits. Grease
  the base of a loose-bottomed or spring-sided 18 cm/7 in flan
  tin, line it with baking paper and press the mixture into it. Chill
  for 1 hour.
- Meanwhile, whip the cream until it is firm but not stiff. Add the
  fromage frais and mascarpone and blend gently until the
  mixture is smooth. Add the caster sugar and two-thirds of the
  raspberries and mix well. Spoon the raspberry mixture into the
  biscuit base. Chill for at least 3 hours.
- Make a raspberry sauce with the remaining raspberries,
  retaining a few for decoration, by pressing them through a
  sieve to make a purée and then stirring in the honey and lemon
  juice. Either pour the sauce over the top of the cheesecake or
  serve it separately.

Shortcrust pastry   makes enough to line a 22 cm/9 in tart tin

magic ingredient... white flour

If you are using white flour in this shortcrust pastry, your body will
receive a good non-dairy source of calcium, the nutrient that maintains
bones and teeth. If you want to make a larger amount of pastry, increase
the quantities of flour and butter proportionately (for 350 g/12 oz flour,
for example, you will need 175 g/6 oz butter).

175 g/6 oz plain white or wholemeal flour
pinch of salt
75 g/3 oz butter, refrigerated
chilled water

- Sift the flour and salt into a bowl and grate in the butter
  straight from the fridge. Rub the butter into the flour using
  your fingertips, handling the ingredients as little as possible.
  Stirring with a knife, add just enough ice-cold water to bind the
  mixture together. Wrap in greaseproof paper and chill in the
  fridge for at least 20 minutes.
- Roll out the pastry on a floured surface and then line the tart
  tin with it. Chill the tin in the fridge for 20 to 30 minutes.
- Preheat the oven to 200°C/400°F/gas mark 6.
- Cut a circle of greaseproof paper to fit the pastry case. Place
  the greaseproof paper in the pastry case and cover it with
  baking beans. Bake in the oven for about 10 to 15 minutes,
  then remove the paper and baking beans and bake for a
  further 5 to 10 minutes.

Blackberry & blueberry fool   serves 4

magic ingredient...blackberries

Not only does this dessert taste wonderful, but it also has high vitamin C
and betacarotene contents. The blackberries furthermore contain
potassium, the nutrient that helps to reduce bloating caused by PMT by
lessening the level of sodium in the body.

150 g/5 oz blueberries
225 g/8 oz blackberries
60 g/2½ oz unsalted butter
100 g/3½ oz caster sugar
3 eggs, well beaten
125 ml/4 fl oz double cream, or half cream and half thick
  Greek-style yoghurt
1 sprig mint (optional)

- Set a few of the blueberries and blackberries aside for
  decoration.
- Crush the blueberries and blackberries in a mortar, using a
  pestle. Turn them into a heatproof bowl and add the butter and
  sugar. Place the bowl over a saucepan of simmering water,
  making sure that the base of the bowl doesn't touch the water.
  Cook over a medium heat, stirring constantly with a wooden
  spoon until the butter and sugar have melted together and
  then beat in the eggs. Continue to cook for about 10 to 15
  minutes, stirring frequently, until the mixture thickens
  considerably. Rub the mixture through a sieve into a bowl,
  leave it to cool and then cover and chill.
- Whip the cream until it is thick, but not too stiff, and fold it
  into the blueberry mixture. If you are using half cream and half
  yoghurt, add the yoghurt to the mixture at this stage.
- Spoon the fool into tall glasses and decorate with a few of the
  reserved berries and perhaps a sprig of mint. Chill the glasses
  until you are ready to serve the dish.

Mango, coconut, lemon-grass & lime dressing   serves 10--12

magic ingredient...mango

Mango contains high levels of vitamin C, a powerful antioxidant that has
many beneficial properties, not least its ability to help wounds to heal
quickly. This piquant dressing can either be served immediately or be kept
in the fridge for three or four days until needed.

200 g/7 oz over-ripe mango, peeled, stoned and roughly
  chopped
100 ml/3½ fl oz coconut milk
4 stalks fresh lemon grass, finely chopped
grated zest and juice of 2 limes
4 dried kaffir lime leaves
1 teaspoons sweet chilli sauce
2 tablespoons olive oil
salt and freshly ground black pepper

- Liquidise all of the ingredients until smooth, ideally using a
  hand-held blender, and then pass the dressing through a fine
  sieve. Season to taste with salt and pepper.

ideas for entertaining

As we struggle to cope with the stresses of modern life, it is easy to lose sight of the leisurely, sensory aspects of eating. Sitting down to enjoy a tasty meal can be a truly voluptuous activity, especially if you share the experience with your friends or family. It is important to remember that one of the best ways in which to glean the most enjoyment and satisfaction from eating is to titillate the mouth, eyes and nose. Meals that have a high organoleptic quality stimulate more than one sense – that is, they look appetising and incorporate a variety of textures, tastes, colours and smells. Such meals are far more likely to excite all of your senses than boring-looking, bland-tasting foods that you feel you should eat rather than actively wanting to.

I believe that we should banish low-fat, reduced-calorie foods from our diets – it's far more satisfying to eat smaller amounts of wonderful-tasting, fresh foods like butter, cream, full-fat cheeses and biscuits. Any food can be healthy if it is eaten correctly, which is why you'll find cream, as well as other ingredients that were once considered to be unhealthy, in my dishes. Most foods – even chocolate and creamy sauces – can be enjoyed if you eat small amounts of them and instead rely on fibre-providers (such as vegetables, fruits, pulses and wholegrain foods such as wholemeal bread) to provide your stomach with bulk. Not only have I used ingredients that are naturally low in fat and sugar in my dishes, but I have also combined higher-calorie ingredients such as olive oil, butter and cream with high-fibre, lower-calorie foods. Combining ingredients like these make the finished dishes simultaneously delicious, satisfying and healthy.

This section would not be complete without mentioning alcohol, which has many nutritional benefits. Alcohol not only encourages the body to produce high-density lipoprotein (HDL), the 'good' form of cholesterol, but also provides your body with powerful antioxidants, which are thought to reduce the incidence of atherosclerosis and are furthermore believed to have cancer-fighting properties (although further research still

needs to be carried out in this area). Too much alcohol can, however, cause weight gain and mood crashes, as well as more serious diseases such as cirrhosis of the liver.

The best way to maximise the advantages that alcohol has to offer without suffering from the disadvantages is to make sure that you don't drink more than 28 units a week if you are a man and 21 units if you are a women (a unit being a glass of wine, half a pint of lager or a single shot of spirits). Ideally, you should not drink alcohol on an empty stomach, because this will cause your blood-sugar and energy levels to fluctuate; drinking alcohol after you have eaten something will enable your body to metabolise it slowly. Before you enjoy a pre-supper drink, have a couple of pieces of fruit and plenty of water (the fibre in the fruit, when activated by the water, will help your stomach to retain the alcohol for longer, thereby preventing your blood-sugar levels from plummeting and your appetite from increasing dramatically). As with food, learning to exploit the positive properties of alcohol and to avoid its negative side effects is what my nutritional philosophy is about.

Entertaining shouldn't just be an activity for adults to enjoy – encouraging children to partake in a leisurely meal that isn't rushed or overshadowed by TV, one that is focused around

sitting and enjoying favourite foods, can ultimately teach them
a valuable life skill – to appreciate food rather than seeing food
simply as fuel. It also pays dividends if you can involve children
in the preparation of meals – if they know how foods are
prepared, they are far more likely to feel inspired and able to
cook for themselves when they're older. Cooking is so much
about inspiration and confidence, rather than pure culinary
skills. If we can teach the next generation to cook and to eat in
a healthy way, many diet-related diseases will find it hard to
take hold in the population of the new millennium.

Chilled roasted tomato soup   serves 4

magic ingredient... tomatoes

Tomatoes contain high levels of lycopene and vitamin E, both strong
antioxidants that help to fight disease. You could use a ready-prepared
bouquet garni for this recipe, but by making your own you will reap the
benefits of the flavours of the fresh herbs. Make one with a mixture of any
of the following: thyme, rosemary, parsley, marjoram and a bay leaf tied
up in a muslin bag.

900 g/2 lb vine-ripened tomatoes
2 cloves garlic, peeled and finely chopped
1 medium-sized onion, finely chopped
3 tablespoons olive oil
2 carrots, finely chopped
2 stalks celery, finely chopped
600 ml/1 pint chicken or vegetable stock
1 bouquet garni
salt and freshly ground black pepper
1 bunch fresh basil
3 tablespoons mascarpone cheese, beaten until smooth

- Roast the tomatoes on a baking tray under a hot grill until
  charred. When cool enough to handle, remove their skins.
- In a large saucepan, lightly sauté the garlic and onion in a dash
  of olive oil until they are golden. Add the carrots and celery
  and sauté for a further 5 minutes.
- Add the tomatoes, stock and bouquet garni. Bring to the boil,
  cover the saucepan and simmer for 30 minutes.
- Remove the bouquet garni, leave the soup to cool and then
  purée it with a hand-held blender. Season to taste and chill.
- Pound the bunch of basil, with a little olive oil drizzled into it,
  in a mortar and pestle to form a thick but not rigid paste.
- Garnish the chilled soup with a circle of basil paste and a dollop
  of mascarpone cheese.

Raspberry gazpacho   serves 6

magic ingredient... raspberries

The raspberries in this gazpacho soup are packed with vitamin C, the
nutrient which helps to prevent colds and infections. You could substitute
other fruits such as peaches, cherries, currants or even melon to vary the
colour and taste of the gazpacho.

1.5 kg/3 lb fresh, ripe raspberries
85 g/3 oz caster sugar, or more if you like a sweeter flavour
100 ml/3 fl oz good pudding wine, like Muscat de Beaumes-
   de-Venise
3 large passion fruits
2 ripe nectarines, stoned and finely diced
6 mint leaves

- Wash and hull the raspberries and set aside 200 g/7 oz for later
  use. Purée the remaining raspberries with the caster sugar.
  Strain the purée through a fine sieve and then pour in the wine
  and mix well.
- Cut the passion fruits in half and scrape the seeds into the
  raspberry mixture (you may need to loosen them gently with
  your fingers so that they float through the soup).
- Chop the reserved raspberries and mix them into the raspberry
  purée, along with the nectarines. Cover the soup and chill.
  Garnish with mint leaves before serving.

Red mullet with basil pesto   serves 4

magic ingredient... red mullet

Red mullet contains high levels of tryptophan, the amino acid that
encourages the brain to produce the endorphins, noradrenaline and
serotonin, making this a mood-enhancing and delicious dish.

3 cloves garlic
50 g/2 oz pine nuts
50 g/2 oz bunch fresh basil
50 g/2 oz bunch fresh, flat-leaved parsley
6 tablespoons olive oil
salt and freshly ground black pepper
4 small red mullet, with livers, cleaned and scaled
2 tablespoons olive oil
2 lemons (slice 1 lemon as a garnish)

- Make the pesto by pounding together the garlic and pine nuts
  in a mortar and pestle. Tear the basil and flat-leaved-parsley
  leaves from their stalks and add them to the garlic mixture,
  pounding well. Add 6 tablespoons of olive oil and stir well.
- Season the red mullet with salt and pepper and then sauté
  them in 2 tablespoons of olive oil for about 7 minutes, turning
  once, until the fish are cooked, but not dry.
- Place the fish on a warmed serving plate and squeeze the juice
  of 1 lemon over them. Spoon a little of the pesto over the fish
  and garnish with lemon slices.

Roasted halibut with capers   serves 4

magic ingredient... halibut

Halibut is packed with essential amino acids, the building blocks of protein
that not only form healthy muscles and repair damaged ones, but also
fortify the immune system. A large, green leafy salad makes a wonderful
accompaniment to this dish.

1 large bunch flat-leaved parsley, chopped
2 tablespoons capers, drained and rinsed
2 shallots, finely chopped
juice of 2 limes
5 tablespoons olive oil
salt and freshly ground black pepper
1 halibut, about 900 g/2 lb in weight, gutted and cleaned, or
  4 halibut steaks weighing 225 g/8 oz each

- First make a dressing by mixing together the parsley, capers,
  shallots and lime juice and then adding the olive oil, salt and
  pepper.
- Preheat the grill until it is very hot.
- Place the halibut under the grill for 5 minutes. Turn the fish
  over and grill it for another 5 minutes (don't let it dry out).
- Transfer the halibut to a serving plate and pour over the
  prepared dressing.

Mackerel with roasted tomatoes & thyme   serves 4

magic ingredient... mackerel

Mackerel is rich in two very beneficial fish oils: omega-3 and omega-6 fatty acids. These oils help to increase the levels of 'good' cholesterol, as well as to decrease the levels of 'bad' cholesterol, in the body. Mackerel also contains linoleic, linolenic and arachidonic acid — three fatty acids that play a vital part in repairing nerve cells. Serve the mackerel with either a green leafy salad or my asparagus and lemon salad.

900 g/2 lb plum tomatoes
4 mackerel
1 bunch fresh thyme
2 lemons, thickly sliced
dash of olive oil
4 bay leaves
2 glasses dry white wine
125 g/4 oz black olives, chopped
salt and freshly ground black pepper

- Place the tomatoes in water that has just gone off the boil for a few minutes and then leave them to rest in cold water. The skin should have cracked enough for you to remove it, as well as the seeds, by hand. Cut the tomatoes in half.
- Preheat the oven to 220°C/425°F/gas mark 7.
- Slice open, gut and clean the mackerel if this has not already been done. Stuff each of the mackerel with 2 sprigs of thyme and 2 slices of lemon and drizzle a little olive oil over the top. Lay a bay leaf on top of each fish. Place in a lightly greased, oven-proof dish and bake in the oven for 7 minutes.
- Pour the white wine over the mackerel and then place the plum tomatoes and olives on top of each fish. Season with salt and pepper. Bake in the oven for a further 7 to 10 minutes, depending on the size of the mackerel.
- Chill and then garnish the fish with sprigs of fresh thyme.

Left: Mackerel with roasted tomatoes and thyme

Sardines stuffed with sultanas   serves 6

magic ingredient... sardines

Sardines contain very high levels of the beneficial fish oils omega-3 and omega-6 fatty acids, which assist the body to rid itself of 'bad' cholesterol. These fish oils also help to soothe the symptoms of rheumatoid arthritis, as well as improving such skin problems as psoriasis.

1 kg/2¼ lb large sardines, heads removed, split and boned
salt and freshly ground black pepper
dash of olive oil
12 tablespoons wholemeal breadcrumbs
50 g/2 oz pine kernels
60 g/2¼ oz sultanas
6 salted anchovies, soaked and chopped, or 12 fillets tinned in
  oil, drained and chopped
450 g/1 lb spinach, sweated in a little olive oil
pinch of fresh nutmeg, grated
⅛ teaspoon ground cloves
2 tablespoons fresh tarragon, chopped
2 tablespoons fresh, flat leaved parsley, chopped
2 shallots, finely chopped
zest of 1 lemon
juice of 2 lemons
6 bay leaves

- Preheat the oven to 200°C/400°F/gas mark 6.
- Season the sardines with salt and pepper. Heat the olive oil in a frying pan and add the breadcrumbs. Brown the breadcrumbs slightly and then add the pine kernels and sultanas.
- Remove the breadcrumb mixture from the pan and place it in a bowl with the anchovies, spinach, nutmeg, ground cloves, tarragon, parsley, shallots, lemon zest and juice. Using your hands, mix all of the ingredients together to make the stuffing.
- Place a little of the stuffing on each sardine and then roll up the fish, starting at the fat end so that the tail sticks up.
- Place the sardines in a lightly oiled gratin dish. Tear the bay leaves over the top of the fish and bake in the oven for 15 minutes, until the fish is cooked, but still moist.

Sea bream in a saffron & ginger sauce   serves 4

magic ingredient... ginger

The ginger in this sauce is a settling ingredient that acts swiftly to calm a stressed and complaining digestive system. Take care when de-seeding and chopping the chilli pepper, because the seeds and juice can cause a burning sensation if they come into contact with your eyes.

4 cloves garlic, chopped
1 fresh red chilli pepper, de-seeded and finely chopped
1 tablespoon olive oil
450 g/1 lb vine-ripened tomatoes, peeled, de-seeded and
  roughly chopped
5 cm/2 in piece fresh root ginger, peeled and finely grated
4 saffron strands, steeped in 2 tablespoons hot water
1 teaspoon brown sugar
salt and freshly ground black pepper
4 sea bream, weighing 225 g/8 oz each, skinned and gutted
juice of 1 lemon

- Sauté the garlic and chilli in the olive oil for 1 or 2 minutes, or until they are soft. Add the tomatoes, ginger, saffron, sugar, salt and pepper. Simmer for 10 minutes.
- Add the sea bream to the pan and simmer for a further 10 to 12 minutes.
- Transfer the fish to serving plates and spoon the sauce around the edge. Squeeze a little lemon juice over each fish and serve at once.

Smoked haddock with a lentil salad   serves 4

magic ingredient... lentils

When in the presence of water, the high-fibre lentils served with the
smoked haddock will help to maintain the health of your gut by enabling
waste products to pass smoothly through the bowel.

175g/6 oz brown lentils
1 litre/35 fl oz water
1 medium-sized onion, finely chopped
1 clove garlic, finely chopped
75 g/3 oz carrots, finely chopped
½ bulb fennel, finely chopped
2 tablespoons fresh parsley, finely chopped
1 tablespoon olive oil
1 tablespoon red wine vinegar
salt and freshly ground black pepper
4 medium-sized pieces smoked haddock
2 limes

- Place the lentils in a large pan and pour the water over the top. Bring to the boil, cover and simmer for 30 to 35 minutes, or until the lentils are soft, but not mushy. Drain well and allow the lentils to cool to room temperature.
- Preheat the grill to a medium heat.
- Transfer the lentils to a serving bowl and then mix them with the onion, garlic, carrots, fennel, parsley, olive oil and vinegar. Season to taste.
- Place the haddock under the grill for approximately 7 minutes, or until the fish is cooked, but not dry.
- To serve, place a helping of lentil salad on each plate and top with a piece of haddock. Squeeze the limes over the fish and serve immediately.

Smoked haddock & rocket tart   serves 6

magic ingredient... smoked haddock

Smoked haddock is packed with low-fat protein and also contains the
antioxidant mineral selenium, which maintains a healthy liver. Rocket is
readily available, but if you can't find any use watercress as an alternative.

350 g/12 oz smoked haddock
300 ml/10 fl oz semi skimmed milk
25 g/1 oz butter
1 small onion, finely chopped
1 stick celery, finely chopped
25 g/1 oz plain flour
salt and freshly ground black pepper
¼ nutmeg, grated
1 bunch rocket or watercress, finely chopped
2 eggs, beaten
275 g/10 oz shortcrust pastry (see page 94), baked blind
2 tablespoons Parmesan cheese, freshly grated

- Preheat the oven to 190°C/375°F/gas mark 5.
- Place the haddock and milk in a saucepan and bring to the boil, then reduce the heat and simmer very gently for 10 minutes. Cool and drain the fish, reserving the milk mixture. Skin the fish and flake it into a bowl.
- Heat the butter in a saucepan, add the onion and celery and cook until they have softened. Stir in the flour and cook for a couple of minutes, then add the reserved milk a little at a time, stirring it in with a wooden spoon, until the sauce has thickened. Season to taste with salt, pepper and nutmeg.
- Remove the saucepan from the heat and stir the sauce into the fish, adding the rugula or watercress and beaten eggs. Pour the filling into the prepared pastry case and sprinkle the Parmesan cheese over the top.
- Bake in the oven for 25 to 30 minutes, or until the tart has risen and has a golden-brown crust. Leave it to cool slightly and then transfer it to a serving plate.

Poached trout   serves 4

magic ingredient... trout

Trout contains high levels of protein, the nutrient that plays an important part in repairing damaged muscles. An oily fish, trout also contains beneficial oils that may help to alleviate such chronic skin disorders as psoriasis by reducing inflammation.

50 g/2 oz butter
500 g/1 lb 2 oz potatoes, peeled and thinly sliced
1 onion, peeled and thinly sliced
salt and freshly ground black pepper
250 ml/9 fl oz fish stock
1 sprig thyme
1 clove garlic, crushed
1 bay leaf
1 large trout, about 1 kg/2 lb 4 oz, gutted
1 tablespoon peanut oil

- Preheat the oven to 220°C/425°F/gas mark 7.
- Butter an ovenproof dish and arrange the sliced vegetables over the bottom. Season with salt and pepper. Pour the stock over the vegetables and arrange the thyme, garlic and bay leaf on top. Bake the vegetables in the oven for 20 minutes.
- Remove the dish from the oven and lay the trout on top of the vegetables. Coat the trout with the peanut oil and season again if necessary. Return the dish to the oven for a further 15 minutes, or until the trout is cooked. Serve immediately.

Smoked salmon & vegetable terrine   serves 4

magic ingredient... smoked salmon

Smoked salmon contains high levels of the fatty acids omega-3 and omega-6, beneficial fish oils that can help to alleviate and prevent muscle cramps and period pains. This terrine is delicious served either hot or cold.

1 green cabbage, leaves separated, washed, stalks removed
8 very tender small leeks, thinly sliced
600 g/1 lb 4 oz spinach, washed, drained and chopped
2 eggs
300 ml/10 fl oz milk
salt and freshly ground black pepper
dash of olive oil
225 g/8 oz smoked salmon
4 tomatoes
juice of ½ lemon

- Blanch leaves for 1 minute in boiling, salted water to soften slightly. Drain well and gently dry them with a paper towel.
- Cook leeks in boiling, salted water for 4 minutes then drain.
- Sweat the spinach in its own moisture for 4 minutes and then drain it well, pressing out any excess liquid.
- Beat together the eggs and milk, stir in the leeks and spinach and season to taste.
- Preheat the oven to 180°C/350°F/gas mark 4. Lightly oil a terrine dish and cover the base and sides with the cabbage leaves. Continue to fill the base of the dish with the leaves until the dish is half full. Cover the leaves with the smoked salmon.
- Cover the salmon with the leek-and-spinach mixture and place a sheet of aluminium foil over the top of the dish. Place the dish in a bain-marie in the oven for 1 hour.
- Blanch tomatoes and remove skins. Cut the tomatoes in half and remove seeds. Place in a liquidiser with lemon juice and liquidise. Season to taste.
- When cooled, turn out the terrine on to a serving dish. Cut into slices about 1 cm/½ in thick and serve with the tomato sauce.

Prawn & saffron risotto   serves 4

magic ingredient... prawns

Prawns are full of zinc, the nutrient that helps to strengthen the immune
system, boosts the libido and also guards against infertility. In addition,
the risotto rice used in this dish is rich in carbohydrates, which provide
the body with energy.

50 g/2 oz butter
3 shallots, finely chopped
2 cloves garlic
few strands of saffron, steeped in tablespoon hot water
350 g/12 oz risotto rice
1 glass dry white wine
900 ml/1½ pints fresh fish or chicken stock
50 g/2 oz Parmesan cheese, finely grated, plus some shavings
   to garnish
32 shelled prawns or langoustine (Dublin Bay if possible)
salt and freshly ground black pepper
juice of 1 lemon
2 tablespoons flat-leaved parsley, chopped

- Melt half of the butter in a large frying pan and sauté the
  shallots and garlic until theybecome clear and start to turn
  golden brown. Add the saffron and rice and stir for 5 minutes,
  or until all of the grains have been warmed through. Pour
  the wine into the pan and cook until it has been absorbed by
  the rice.
- Heat up the stock in a separate pan and leave it to simmer.
  Gradually add the stock a cup at a time to the rice, stirring
  constantly, being careful not to add more stock until the last
  cupful has been absorbed. Add Parmesan cheese and stir well.
- Meanwhile, heat the remaining butter in a separate frying pan
  and quickly sauté the prawns. Season them with black pepper
  and a little salt, along with a dash of lemon juice.
- Place the risotto rice on a large, warmed serving dish and
  arrange the prawns over the top. Garnish with shavings of
  Parmesan cheese and chopped parsley and sprinkle the
  remaining lemon juice over the top.

Pasta bows with spring vegetables   serves 4

magic ingredient... pasta

Pasta is a settling food that is both easy to digest and induces sleep
(because it contains starch it encourages the body to relax). This recipe is
delicious served either hot or cold; it also keeps very well in a lunchbox.

4 courgettes, sliced
salt and freshly ground black pepper
100 g/3½ oz fresh or frozen broad beans
1 bunch asparagus spears
50 g/2 oz frozen peas
3 tablespoons olive oil
1 clove garlic, crushed
¼ teaspoon cayenne pepper
450 g/1 lb pasta bows (farfalle)
1 tablespoon mint, chopped
2 tablespoons parsley, chopped
Parmesan cheese, freshly grated

- Place the courgettes in a colander and sprinkle them with salt
  to draw out the excess water. Leave for 30 minutes and then
  rinse with cold water.
- Steam the beans, asparagus and peas until they are al dente.
- Heat the olive oil in a large frying pan and sauté the garlic. Add
  the cayenne pepper and courgettes and sauté for a further 5
  minutes.
- Meanwhile, boil the pasta until it is al dente, then drain it well.
- Tip the pasta into the frying pan and add the mint, parsley,
  beans, asparagus and peas. Mix well, season to taste and
  sprinkle with Parmesan cheese.

Chargrilled squid with limes & chilli & a tomato salad   serves 2–4

magic ingredient... limes

Limes contain high levels of vitamin C and bioflavonoids, powerful
antioxidants in the juice and zest that combat the damage caused by free
radicals, including cancer, heart disease and arthritis.

Tomato salad
200 g/7 oz vine-ripened tomatoes
juice of 2 limes
1 medium-hot red chilli, finely chopped
1 clove garlic, finely chopped
1 shallot, finely chopped
3 tablespoons fresh coriander, finely chopped
salt and freshly ground black pepper

Dressing
juice of 2 limes
3 tablespoons light brown sugar
1 tablespoon Thai fish sauce
½ teaspoon red chilli, chopped
1 teaspoon chilli sauce
zest of 1 lime

Squid
500 g/1 lb squid, cleaned and cut into thick strips
dash of olive oil

- First make the tomato salad by roughly chopping the tomatoes. Add the juice of the limes and the chopped chilli, garlic, shallot, coriander, salt and pepper. Leave to marinate while you make the rest of the dish.
- To make the dressing, first put the lime juice, sugar, fish sauce, chilli and chilli sauce in a small pan and place over a gentle heat until the mixture comes to the boil. Once the sugar has dissolved and the dressing has turned a golden, syrupy colour, remove the pan from the heat (it will burn easily).
- Thread the squid strips on to skewers and drizzle a little olive oil over them. Grill the skewers either on a barbecue or under a hot grill, for 1 or 2 minutes. Brush the squid pieces with the dressing as they are cooking (the dressing will give them a golden, glazed appearance. Once they are cooked, remove the squid pieces from the skewers and serve them sprinkled with the lime zest accompanied by the tomato salad.

Left: Chargrilled squid with limes and chilli and a tomato salad

Salmon with chicory, tomatoes & basil   serves 4

magic ingredient... salmon

Salmon contains the nerve-repairing nutrients linoleic acid, linolenic acid and arachidonic acid, essential fatty acids contained in the body's cell membranes and prostaglandins that may help to modify the symptoms of multiple sclerosis.

2 heads chicory
1 large tomato
1 stem fresh basil
1 tablespoon olive oil
juice of 2 lemons
salt and freshly ground black pepper
600 g/1 lb 4 oz fillets of salmon, thinly sliced

- Slice the leaves of the chicory thinly. Scald the tomato by placing it in boiling water for 1 or 2 minutes until the skin cracks. Lift the tomato from the water with a spoon and peel off the skin. Sauté the skin with 4 basil leaves in a dash of olive oil for 2 minutes.
- Remove the pips from the tomato and crush the flesh. Make a dressing with the lemon juice, olive oil, salt and pepper.
- Add a dash of olive oil to a frying pan and brown the salmon fillets on one side only over a high heat for 5 minutes. Transfer the fish to a serving plate and surround it with the chicory leaves and tomato flesh. Sprinkle the dressing over the fish and decorate it with the sautéed tomato skin and basil. Garnish with some freshly torn basil before serving.

Crispy duck with nectarines & cashew nuts   serves 4

magic ingredient... cashew nuts

Cashew nuts contain high levels of zinc, a libido-boosting nutrient, and nectarines are rich in vitamin C, a powerful immune-system-fortifying antioxidant. If you can't buy fresh nectarines you could use tinned ones instead, but fresh are far superior, so try to make this salad when they are in season.

4 duck breasts, each weighing 175 g/6 oz
salt
2 tablespoons runny honey
3 tablespoons light soy sauce
2 tablespoons balsamic vinegar
1 cm/½ in piece root ginger, finely chopped
4 tablespoons olive oil
1 small bag salad leaves or 8 large crisp lettuce leaves
3 spring onions, finely chopped
4 fresh nectarines, stoned and sliced
50 g/2 oz cashew nuts

- Dry and trim the duck breasts, then lightly score their skins with a sharp knife. Season each breast with a little salt.
- Place a large, non-stick frying pan over a moderate heat, add the duck breasts, skin side down, and cook for 2 to 3 minutes. Turn them over and cook for a further 2 to 3 minutes. (The time given is for medium-rare duck, which is pink in the centre. If you prefer it well done, cook it for 5 to 6 minutes on each side.) Transfer the duck to a plate and keep warm.
- To make the dressing, mix together in a small bowl or screw-topped jar the honey, soy sauce, vinegar and ginger. Add the olive oil and mix thoroughly.
- Arrange the salad leaves, spring onions and nectarines on a large plate. Slice the duck and arrange the slices over the top of the salad. Sprinkle with cashew nuts and drizzle some of the dressing over the top. Serve the remaining dressing separately.

Grilled poussins with herbs & lemon coats   serves 4

magic ingredient... poussins

Poussins are small, lean protein-rich birds; their inclusion in this dish will help your body to build up strong muscles. Digestive enzymes in the stomach break protein down into amino acids, which are then transported around the body in the bloodstream.

4 tablespoons fresh rosemary, chopped
4 tablespoons fresh basil, torn
4 tablespoons fresh marjoram, chopped
4 tablespoons fresh sage, chopped
50 g/2 oz butter
1 tablespoon Dijon mustard
1 clove garlic, finely chopped
4 poussins or baby chickens, giblets removed
8 lemons, cut into quarters
salt and freshly ground black pepper
citron confit, very thinly sliced, to garnish (optional)

- Preheat the oven to 200°C/400°F/gas mark 6.
- Place the rosemary, basil, marjoram and sage in a bowl and mix in the butter, mustard and garlic.
- Divide the herb butter into four portions and, using your hands, insert it under the skin of each poussin. (You should find that the skin comes away from the flesh if you loosen it carefully – try not to pierce the skin.)
- Arrange the poussins in an ovenproof baking tray. Place a lemon quarter into each of the poussins and then tuck the remaining lemon quarters around them. Sprinkle with salt and pepper.
- Place the poussins in the oven and roast them for 20 minutes, basting them at least once. Check that the meat is cooked by piercing it a sharp knife; if it is done the juices should run clear. If you are using them, garnish the poussins with slices of citron confit before serving.

Noodles with red peppers, chicken & cashew nuts   serves 4

magic ingredient... red peppers

Red peppers are rich in betacarotene, an antioxidant that the body
converts into vitamin A which helps to reduce the incidence of cancer, as
well as promoting growth, good vision and healthy skin.

dash of olive oil
4 red peppers, cored, de-seeded and chopped into quarters
8 shallots, peeled and halved
3 cloves garlic, peeled but left whole
1 teaspoon fresh thyme leaves
1 teaspoon fresh rosemary leaves, chopped
3 chicken breasts, sliced into thin strips
1 teaspoon olive oil
350 g/12 oz dried noodles
50 g/2 oz cashew nuts
salt and freshly ground black pepper

- Preheat the oven to 200°C/400°F/gas mark 6.
- Brush a roasting tin with a little olive oil. Arrange the peppers, shallots and garlic in the tin and sprinkle with the thyme and rosemary leaves. Bake in the oven for 10 minutes. Add the chicken and bake for a further 10 minutes, basting the vegetables occasionally.
- Bring a large saucepan of water to the boil and add the salt, olive oil and noodles. Boil the noodles for about 10 minutes, or until they are *al dente*.
- When the chicken is cooked and the vegetables are soft and brown around the edges, remove them from the roasting tin. Drain the noodles and combine them with the chicken mixture. Stir in the cashew nuts and season with salt and pepper.

Rosemary vegetables   serves 4

magic ingredient... vegetables

All of the vegetables in this recipe are high in fibre, which assists the body
to absorb nutrients gradually. They can either be served on their own,
with charcuterie or stirred into pasta.

4 tablespoons olive oil, plus a little extra
4 large baking potatoes, scrubbed clean
salt and freshly ground black pepper
3 tablespoons fresh rosemary leaves, chopped
450 g/1 lb baby carrots, scrubbed
4 small shallots, peeled and roots removed
2 large courgettes, cleaned and cut into quarters
450 g/1 lb asparagus

- Preheat the oven to 200°C/400°F/gas mark 6.
- Grease a large baking tray with olive oil. Cut the potatoes into quarters. Drizzle the potatoes with olive oil and sprinkle salt, pepper and the rosemary leaves over the top.
- Roast the potatoes in the oven for 30 minutes, or until they are starting to soften. Add the carrots and shallots and stir, adding a little more olive oil if necessary (make sure that the rosemary is evenly distributed among all of the vegetables). Return to the oven for a further 10 minutes.
- Add the courgettes to the vegetables and stir, making sure that they are coated in oil, and then roast for a further 10 to 15 minutes.
- Add the asparagus and roast for a further 10 to 15 minutes, or until all of the vegetables are soft.

Left: Noodles with red peppers, chicken and cashew nuts

One-pot Moroccan turkey   serves 6

magic ingredient... turkey

Turkey contains zinc, a nutrient that not only boosts the libido, but also improves problem skin, eczema and psoriasis by reducing inflammation and encouraging the healing process.

110 g/4 oz blanched almonds
4 substantial turkey pieces such as thighs or legs
2 tablespoons olive oil
1 large onion, finely chopped
2 cloves garlic, finely chopped
2 tablespoons tomatoes, peeled
1 tablespoon tomato purée
½ teaspoon ground ginger
2 teaspoons ground cinnamon
2 strands saffron or ½ teaspoon turmeric
2 tablespoons clear honey
2 tablespoons toasted sesame seeds

- Brown the blanched almonds by arranging them on baking sheet and placing it under a moderately hot grill for a minute or two – watch the almonds carefully, as they can easily catch fire – or dry-fry in a non-stick frying pan.
- Place all ingredients, except almonds, honey and sesame seeds, in a large pan. Cover and cook gently for about 40 minutes, stirring occasionally, until the flesh starts to fall off the bones.
- Remove the turkey pieces from the pan, strip the meat from the bones, place the meat on a plate and keep warm. Continue to cook the sauce until it is sizzling and thick, stirring constantly. Once it has caramelised fully, add the honey and then the turkey. Heat through thoroughly.
- Drizzle the turkey with a little sauce and garnish with the almonds and sesame seeds.

Cumin-roasted lamb   serves 2

magic ingredient... lamb

It is important that we all eat a source of protein, such as lamb, every day. There can be few tastier ways to provide your body with the amino acids that it needs to build up and maintain its strength.

1.5 kg/3 lb shoulder of lamb, scored with a sharp knife to reveal large cuts
6 cloves garlic
½ teaspoon cumin seeds
6 tablespoons mint leaves, finely chopped
juice of 2 limes
salt and freshly ground black pepper
2 tablespoons olive oil
1 glass light red wine or stock

- Place the lamb in a roasting tin. Put the garlic, cumin seeds, mint leaves, lime juice, salt and pepper in a blender. Blend for a few seconds, adding a little olive oil as you do so, to make a medium-thick paste.
- Rub the paste into the lamb, making sure that it penetrates the cuts. Place the lamb in a cool place to marinate for a couple of hours (you may need to check that the paste has not run off the meat – if it has, baste it again).
- Preheat the oven to 200°C/400°F/gas mark 6. Place the lamb in the oven for 15 to 30 minutes (roast it for a few more minutes if you like your lamb well done). Remove the lamb from the oven and allow it to rest for 15 minutes before carving it.
- To make the gravy, place the roasting tin on top of the stove, pour in the wine or stock and bring to the boil. Stir well and allow the gravy to cook for a couple of minutes. Season to taste and serve with the roast lamb.

Chicken skewers with a lime & mint dressing serves 2

magic ingredient... chicken

The chicken in this recipe is rich in lean protein, making it an ideal
ingredient if you are watching your weight. After you have marinated the
chicken this dish is extremely quick to make.

2 large chicken thighs, boned
zest and juice of 2 limes
leaves of 8 sprigs mint, finely chopped
1 tablespoon dark soy sauce
2 cloves garlic, finely chopped
salt and freshly ground black pepper

- Chop the chicken meat into 7.5 cm/3 in pieces and place them in a non-metallic bowl with the rest of the ingredients. Leave to marinate for 1 or 2 hours.
- Push the chicken pieces on to skewers. Place the skewers on a preheated chargrill, or under a moderately heated grill, for approximately 3 to 4 minutes, or until the chicken has turned golden brown and is cooked throughout. Turn regularly and baste the chicken with the dressing.

Chicken baked in spicy yoghurt serves 8

magic ingredient... yoghurt

Yoghurt contains magnesium, a mineral that, in conjunction with calcium,
assists the body to build up and maintain healthy bones and teeth.
Note that you will need to marinate the chicken for 24 hours. This dish is
delicious served either warm or cold.

1 large, free-range chicken, 2.25 kg/5 lb, skin removed
3 medium-sized onions, finely chopped
15 cloves garlic, finely chopped
13 cm/5 in piece fresh root ginger, peeled and finely chopped
3 green chillies, de-seeded and finely chopped
75 g/3 oz blanched almonds, roughly chopped
600 ml/1 pint natural yoghurt
1 tablespoon ground cumin
1 tablespoon ground coriander seeds
½ teaspoon cayenne pepper
1 teaspoon seeds from green cardamom pods
1 teaspoon garam masala
1 teaspoon salt
2 tablespoons olive oil
5 cloves
1 cinnamon stick
5 peppercorns
handful each of sultanas and flaked almonds
2 tablespoons fresh coriander, chopped

- Cut the chicken into eight pieces and make deep cuts in the flesh, using a sharp knife. Arrange the chicken pieces in a glass or ceramic dish.
- Make the yoghurt paste by placing the onions, garlic, ginger, chillies, almonds and half of the yoghurt in a liquidiser and then blending to make a smooth paste.
- Place the rest of the yoghurt in another bowl with the ground cumin, coriander seeds, cayenne pepper, cardamom seeds, garam masala and salt and mix well. Add the paste to the spicy yoghurt and mix thoroughly. Rub the paste into the chicken, being careful to penetrate the cuts. Cover the dish with plastic wrap and refrigerate for 24 hours.
- The following day, preheat the oven to 190°C/375°F/gas mark 5. Heat the olive oil in a frying pan and then add the cloves, cinnamon stick and peppercorns. Warm the spices for 1 minute and then pour the oil over the chicken.
- Cover the chicken with either a lid or foil and bake in the oven for 50 minutes. Ten minutes before the end of the cooking time, sprinkle the chicken with the sultanas and flaked almonds and return it to the oven uncovered. Sprinkle with the chopped coriander and serve.

Pot-roasted lemon chicken   serves 6

magic ingredient...chicken

Chicken contains high levels of protein, a nutrient that helps to keep
energy levels constant and therefore prevents you from becoming
fatigued. You could serve this dish hot, but it is also great served cold,
either with a salad or in a sandwich made with fresh, wholegrain bread.

2 large lemons, the zest grated from 1 lemon
4 tablespoons olive oil
8 stalks tarragon, leaves removed and finely chopped
6 cloves garlic, peeled and finely chopped
salt and freshly ground black pepper
1.8 kg/4 lb free-range chicken, giblets removed
1 glass dry white wine

- Preheat the oven to 180°C/350°F/gas mark 4.
- In a small bowl, mix the lemon zest, olive oil, tarragon, garlic, salt and pepper. Set to one side.
- Slash the flesh of the chicken to enable it to absorb the flavours easily and place in a casserole dish. Cut the lemons in half, insert them into the chicken cavity and rub all of the prepared herby paste over the chicken. Pour the wine over the chicken, cover the dish with a lid and place it in the oven for 1 hour.
- Remove the dish from the oven and turn the chicken over, basting it with the juices as you do so. Return the chicken to the oven for another 30 minutes and then turn it over again so that it is the right way up.
- Remove the lid and return the dish to the oven for a further 20 minutes, or until the skin has turned golden brown (the meat should fall away from the bones when fully cooked).
- Allow chicken to rest before lifting out of the dish to serve.

Garlic & dill dressing   makes 300 ml/10 fl oz

magic ingredient...garlic

Garlic has powerful anti-bacterial properties, while yoghurt is packed with
calcium. This dressing is a good accompaniment to such fish as trout,
sardines and mackerel. It can also be kept covered in the fridge for three
to four days. If you want to make a slightly thicker dressing, add a slice of
fresh bread to the ingredients before blending them.

250 g/9 oz natural yoghurt
2 teaspoons mustard
2 tablespoons fresh dill, chopped
1 clove garlic, chopped
salt and freshly ground black pepper

- Place all of the ingredients, apart from the salt and pepper, in a blender or liquidiser and blend them until smooth. Season to taste with salt and pepper.

Japanese spring rolls   serves 6

magic ingredient... red peppers

Red peppers are rich in betacarotene, a powerful nutrient that prevents
fat from depositing itself in the blood vessels and nurtures the skin, both
functions that gain increasing importance in middle age.

Miso dressing
2 tablespoons barley miso
1 red chilli, de-seeded and finely sliced
200 ml/7 fl oz light soy sauce
1 tablespoon fresh ginger, peeled and finely chopped
2 tablespoons dark brown sugar
juice of 2 limes
100 ml/3 fl oz sesame oil

Spring rolls
2 large aubergines, cut lengthwise into thick strips
salt
4 courgettes, cut lengthwise into thick strips
2 red peppers, de-seeded and cut into thick strips
2 yellow peppers, de-seeded and cut into thick strips
75 g/3 oz fresh shiitake mushrooms, sliced in half
dash of sesame oil
18 large spinach leaves

- Make the miso dressing by mixing all of the ingredients
  together in a bowl. Set it aside while you make the spring rolls.
- Rub the aubergines with salt and place them in a bowl for 30
  minutes to remove their bitterness. Wash them thoroughly to
  remove the salt and then pat them dry with a kitchen towel.
- Brush the aubergines, courgettes, red and yellow peppers and
  mushrooms with a little sesame oil and then chargrill them until
  they are soft and slightly charred.
- Remove the tough veins from the spinach leaves. Place the
  spinach leaves on a flat working surface and arrange a few of
  the chargrilled vegetables on top of each leaf. Roll up the
  leaves carefully (the heat from the vegetables will make the
  spinach leaves rather soft). Secure each roll with a couple of
  cocktail sticks and arrange on a serving plate. Drizzle the little
  of the dressing over each of the spring rolls.

Roasted peppers & tomatoes   serves 4 as a starter

magic ingredient... red peppers

Red peppers contain antioxidants, which help the body to maintain strong
defences against infection and disease.

2 large red peppers
450 g/1 lb red and yellow cherry tomatoes
450 g/1 lb plum tomatoes
6 cloves garlic, peeled
4 shallots, peeled and sliced into quarters
8 sprigs thyme, leaves removed
1 tablespoon fresh oregano
1 large dash of olive oil
salt and freshly ground black pepper
2 teaspoons red wine vinegar
handful of fresh basil leaves, torn

- Preheat the oven to 220°C/425°F/gas mark 7.
- Prepare the peppers by cutting them into quarters and
  removing the stalks and seeds. Arrange them on a baking tray
  with the tomatoes, garlic and shallots. Sprinkle with the thyme,
  oregano, olive oil, salt and pepper.
- Roast the vegetables in the oven for about 35 to 40 minutes,
  or until they are soft and charred at the edges.
- Using a slotted spoon, remove the vegetables from the tray,
  reserving the juices, and transfer to warmed serving plates.
- Heat the reserved juices and vinegar in a small pan for a couple
  of minutes, or until the sauce has thickened. Add the basil
  leaves and season to taste. Drizzle the sauce over the
  vegetables and serve at once.

Poached fresh figs   serves 6

magic ingredient... figs

Figs provide a hefty source of calcium, the essential bone-building
nutrient, and are therefore a wonderful alternative to dairy products if
you are sensitive to lactose or cows'-milk protein.

600 ml/1 pint Italian red wine
225 g/8 oz white sugar
18 fresh, ripe figs

- Place the wine and sugar in a non-aluminum saucepan large
  enough to hold all of the figs in one layer. Warm over a
  medium heat until the sugar has dissolved.
- Holding the figs by their stems, drop them gently into the
  wine-and-sugar mixture. Lower to a gentle heat and simmer for
  7 to 10 minutes, until the figs are tender and deep-brown in
  colour.
- Using a slotted spoon, remove the figs, being careful that they
  don't burst, and transfer them to a serving dish. Reduce the
  syrup for about 6 minutes, or until it has become thick. Pour
  the syrup over the figs and allow the dish to cool to room
  temperature.

Summer fruit bread pudding   serves 6

magic ingredient... summer fruits

The summer fruits in this dessert are packed with vitamin C, a powerful
antioxidant that helps your body to absorb iron. If you are a smoker you
are in danger of depleting your levels of vitamin C and of developing iron-
deficiency anaemia, so boost your intake of this antioxidant with
delectable dishes like this one.

2 eggs
2 egg yolks
3 tablespoons caster sugar
300 ml/10 fl oz milk
300 ml/10 fl oz cream
½ teaspoon vanilla essence
225 g/8 oz soft wholemeal or white rolls
100 g/3½ oz unsalted butter
50 g/2 oz Demerara sugar
700 g/1½ lb berry fruits (plenty of blackberries and raspberries,
*   gooseberries, blackcurrants, strawberries, redcurrants)*
apricot glaze (optional)

- Preheat the oven to 180°C/350°F/gas mark 4.
- Mix together the eggs, egg yolks, caster sugar, milk, cream and
  vanilla essence to make a custard.
- Butter a 1.5 litre/2½ pint pie dish. Cut the rolls in half and
  spread them with butter. Place a layer of bread in the bottom
  of the dish. Scatter with some of the Demerara sugar and the
  fruit mixture and then layer with more bread, sugar and fruit,
  ending with bread. Pour the custard mixture through a sieve
  over the whole of the dish.
- Place in a bain-marie and cook in the oven for 30 to 40
  minutes, or until the custard has set and the top has browned.
  Brush with apricot glaze if you are using it.

Left: Poached fresh figs

Blackberry and plum polenta upside-down pudding   serves 6

magic ingredient... polenta

Polenta is a gluten-free grain that provides the body with a source of slow-release energy while at the same time being gentle on a gluten-sensitive stomach.

450 g/1 lb mixture of plums and blackberries
4 medium eggs
1 vanilla pod, seeds extracted
1 teaspoon green cardamom seeds
50 g/2 oz caster sugar
250 ml/9 fl oz vegetable oil
250 ml/9 fl oz white wine
2½ teaspoons baking powder
120 g/4½ oz quick-cook polenta
4 tablespoons runny honey

- Preheat the oven to 180°C/350°F/gas mark 4.
- Line the base of a deep sponge tin, 25 cm/10 in iwith baking parchment. Cut plums in half and stone. Arrange cut side uppermost over the bottom of the tin. Wash the blackberries, drain well and arrange around the plums.
- Beat together the eggs, vanilla seeds, cardamom seeds and sugar for 2 minutes. Add the oil and wine and beat for 1 minute. Sift the baking powder and polenta and add them to the egg mixture, mixing well.
- Pour the batter over the fruit and bake for 30 minutes.
- Place aluminium foil on top of the pudding and bake for another 30 minutes, until it is cooked. Test by inserting a skewer into it; it should come out clean when you withdraw it.
- Preheat the grill to a medium-to-hot heat and turn out the pudding on to a heatproof plate. Pour the honey over the top and place under the grill to brown off the honey.

Almond torte   serves 6

magic ingredient... almonds

Almonds are full of zinc, an immune-system-boosting nutrient that also helps to clear up spotty skin because it calms inflammation and encourages the healing process.

225 g/8 oz finely ground almonds
110 g/4 oz plain white flour
1 teaspoon cream of tartar
¼ teaspoon salt
6 eggs
225 g/8 oz caster sugar
3 tablespoons amaretto
½ teaspoon vanilla extract
whipped cream, crème fraîche or thick Greek-style yoghurt
raspberries to decorate

- Preheat oven to 170°C/325°F/gas mark 3. Line a round 25 cm/10 in cake tin with greaseproof paper and oil it. Stir together almonds, flour, cream of tartar and salt and set aside.
- Using an electric whisk, whisk the eggs in a heatproof bowl over a pan of hot water (do not let the water boil or come into contact with the base of the bowl) until frothy, creamy in colour and almost fills the bowl.
- Add sugar to the eggs and whisk again until dissolved. Remove from the heat, add the amaretto and vanilla extract, mixing well. Whisk flour mixture into egg mixture, incorporating well.
- Pour batter into prepared tin and bake for 45 minutes, or until a knife inserted into the centre comes out clean.
- Leave to cool then lift it out. Remove the greaseproof paper..
- Once cooled, top with whipped cream, crème fraîche or Greek-style yoghurt and arrange the raspberries on top.

Rhubarb & strawberry crumble   serves 4

magic ingredient... strawberries

Strawberries are rich in the antioxidant vitamin C, making this dish an
irresistible way in which to protect children against developing diseases,
as well as providing their bodies with the nutrients they need for growth.

900 g/2 lb rhubarb, peeled and cut into thick chunks
juice of 1 orange
110 g/4 oz strawberries
75 g/3 oz Demerara sugar

Crumble topping
50 g/2 oz Demerara sugar
110 g/4 oz oats
50 g/2 oz wholewheat flour
50 g/2 oz butter, cut into small cubes

- Preheat the oven to 200°C/400°F/gas mark 6.
- Place the rhubarb and orange juice in a large saucepan and cook until the rhubarb is tender. Transfer to an ovenproof dish and add the strawberries and Demerara sugar.
- To make the crumble topping, mix together the sugar, oats and flour in a bowl. Using the tips of your fingers, rub the butter into the dry ingredients until the mixture resembles crumbs. Top the fruit mixture with the crumble and bake in the oven for 25 minutes, or until the crumble is golden brown.

Summer pudding   serves 6

magic ingredient... summer fruits

The summer fruits in this pudding are packed with potassium, a mineral
that lowers high blood pressure. Because our sodium (salt) intake is
generally high, it is important to counterbalance the sodium by eating
plenty of potassium-rich foods.

6 slices wholemeal bread, crusts removed
1.5 kg/3 lb berry fruits (raspberries, gooseberries, blackberries,
* blackcurrants, stawberries, redcurrants) washed, hulled*
3 tablespoons runny honey
1 tablespoon fresh mint, plus leaves for garnish
juice of 1 orange

- Line the bottom of a 900 ml/1½ pint soufflé dish or pudding basin with one or two slices of bread, covering the base. Line the sides with more bread, cutting it into shape so that the slices fit closely together.
- Place the berries in a wide, heavy-based pan and add the honey. Bring to the boil over a very low heat and cook for 2 to 3 minutes. until the juices have started to run.
- Remove from the heat and set aside 1 or 2 tablespoons of the juice. Add the mint to the berries. Spoon the berries, the remaining juice and orange juice into the prepared dish and tightly cover with the rest of the bread.
- Place a plate that fits inside the dish on top of the pudding and weight it with a heavy tin or jar. Leave to chill for 8 hours.
- Remove the weight and plate. Cover the dish with a serving plate and turn the dish upside down to unmould the pudding. Pour the reserved fruit juice over any parts of the bread that have not been completely soaked and coloured by the berries' juice. Garnish with a few sprigs of mint.

eating on the move

My inspiration for compiling the selection of recipes in this chapter came from having been exposed to lousy catering on trains and planes, which usually left me with a leaden stomach, feeling unsatisfied and generally far from energised at the end of the journey. Our bodies need a regular supply of food and drink in order to maintain even moods and energy levels, as well as healthy constitutions. Indeed, incidences of 'road rage' and in-flight disagreements can often occur because people who haven't eaten or drunk anything for some time are feeling either ravenously hungry or dehydrated or have low blood-sugar levels.

Business people want to be in tiptop form when they arrive at their meetings, while mothers have to be able to cope with children clamouring that they are 'starving' in the back of the car on the way home from school. It is therefore important that you eat and drink regularly, even when you are on the move.

Some people believe that it is far too much trouble to devise strategies for eating healthily when they're on the move. It is certainly tempting to consume whatever is available when you're travelling (like travel sweets in the car or concessionary alcohol on the plane), not necessarily because you're hungry or thirsty, but simply because it's there. Travelling can be boring, and eating and drinking are effective ways in which to alleviate the tedium. We have to remember however, that our bodies are not dustbins that uncomplainingly absorb whatever is thrown into them. On the contrary, our digestive systems require good-quality food and drink to enable the brain, liver, heart muscles and skin – to name just a few organs that are powered by the digestive system – to perform the many functions that we demand of them. Envisage the tiny tablet that makes you feel better when you are under the weather and then compare that to the volume of food that you eat – in terms of both quantity and quality, what you put into your body can therefore have a significant effect on your well-being.

When you are flying or making a long train journey, consider taking along your own nutritious food. Not only will it taste a lot better than commercially produced fare, but it will also benefit, rather than compromise, your health. If you manage to achieve the correct balance between convenience, nutritiousness and satisfaction (which I've aimed to do in this chapter), you'll give your body a nourishing boost and will consequently feel marvellous too.

In nutritional terms, the key to successful travelling is to take the time to plan ahead. I hope that you will be inspired to do so by looking through the recipes that I've included in this chapter. All of these foods can easily be carried around in plastic storage containers or small flasks, while foods such as my sardine and roasted-pepper flan (see page 129) can be eaten with plastic cutlery. Keep in mind that many recipes from the other sections can also be made transportable. My pizza recipes are delicious cold and could not be simpler to pack. All will furthermore last for a reasonable amount of time (pasta salads like my tomato and basil pasta salad – see page 133 – will keep for a few hours) and shouldn't spoil in transit. Above all, they will aid your body to travel smoothly on its journey to good and lasting health.

In addition to food, it is vital that you carry water around with you on your travels (especially when you are flying), in order to keep your body hydrated. Take along a small flask or water bottle in the car, on the train or plane or tuck one into your child's satchel.

Remember that drinking alcohol, especially at altitude, is the worst thing that you can do to your body while you are travelling. Alcohol drastically dehydrates your body, plays havoc with your energy levels and sleeping patterns and will generally have significantly undermined your well-being by the time that you finally arrive at your destination. In addition, drinking alcohol on an empty stomach increases your appetite dramatically (and weight gain is a common problem among travellers). So if you want a drink while you are on the move, keep your alcohol intake to a minimum, drink plenty of water at the same time and try to resist having an alcoholic drink until you eat your meal, a strategy which will cushion the negative effects of the alcohol because it remains in the stomach for longer, where it is metabolised more efficiently than after it has passed into the gut.

Too much caffeine (which is contained in tea, coffee, cola-based drinks and so-called 'sports drinks') will similarly aggravate your energy levels, making it far harder for your body to regulate its circadian rhythms (the rhythms that ensure that you feel sleepy or energetic at the appropriate times). Whether you are on the move or not, stick to just two to three cups of caffeine-containing drinks a day and instead quench your thirst and hydrate your body with water.

All in all, keeping your body well watered when travelling, as well as treating it to nutritious, easy-to-carry foods, will pay dividends, both in the short and the long haul.

Pecorino with celery & walnuts on granary bread   serves 4

magic ingredient... pecorino

Pecorino is a sheeps' cheese which contains high levels of calcium and protein, making it a useful source of these nutrients for people who cannot tolerate cows' milk. It is good for children who have infantile eczema, because it doesn't contain the cows' milk protein that can aggravate this condition.

butter, softened
4 or 8 slices granary bread
150 g/5 oz pecorino cheese, shaved
4 sticks celery, finely chopped
25 g/1 oz walnuts, chopped
salt and freshly ground black pepper

- Lightly butter the bread. Mix the pecorino with the celery and walnuts, season to taste and spread over 4 slices of bread.
- If making to take with you on a trip, top with another slice of bread before wrapping in plastic wrap or placing in a lidded plastic container.

Tuscan bean stew   serves 6

magic ingredient... beans

Beans contain fibre which helps to keep both the digestive system and the heart healthy, as well as aiding the body to resist such diseases as cancer. Although soaking and cooking the beans may seem like a bother, it is worth the effort. Similarly, making your own bouquet garni is more nutritious than buying a ready prepared one.

750 g/1½ lb dried haricot, kidney, cannellini, butter, flageolet,
  aduki or black beans, soaked overnight in cold water, or
  canned beans, drained
1 leek, cleaned and thickly sliced
2 carrots, scrubbed and chopped into thick slices
2 sticks celery, chopped into thick slices
1 bunch fresh rosemary
1 litre/1¾ pints chicken or vegetable stock
1 bouquet garni
50 ml/2 fl oz best-quality Tuscan olive oil
4 fresh sage leaves or 1 teaspoon dried sage
2 cloves garlic, chopped and peeled
salt and freshly ground black pepper
450 g/1 lb canned plum tomatoes, chopped (save the juice)
dash of dry white wine
1 small bunch fresh basil, torn

- If you are using dried beans, after their overnight soaking drain and rinse them thoroughly in cold water.
- Put the beans in a saucepan and cover with cold water. Bring to a fast boil for at least 5 minutes.
- Drain and rinse the bean mixture and return it to the pan. Cover the beans with stock, add the add the leek, carrots, celery, rosemary and bouquet garni, return to the boil and simmer for about 1 hour, or until the beans are tender (cooking time will vary according to the type of bean).
- Heat the oil in another saucepan and add the sage, garlic and a large pinch of black pepper. Sauté for about 5 minutes, or until the garlic is golden brown.
- Add the cooked beans to the pan (if using canned beans, mix them in at this point). Stir the ingredients together and add the tomatoes and their juice. Season to taste with salt and pepper and cover. Simmer gently for about 25 minutes.
- Add a dash of dry white wine and tear the basil into the stew.

Chickpea & feta cheese salad   serves 4

magic ingredient... feta cheese

Feta cheese is rich in calcium, a nutrient that plays an important part in maintaining strong bones. It is also free of cows'-milk protein, which makes it easily digestible by people who have this allergy.

4 tablespoons olive oil
1 red chilli, de-seeded and finely chopped
12 cloves garlic, peeled and finely chopped
4 shallots, peeled and finely chopped
150 ml/5 fl oz cider vinegar
820 g/29 oz tins chickpeas
4 spring onions, finely sliced
8 tablespoons fresh mint, chopped
1 tablespoon sesame oil
8 tablespoons each fresh coriander and flat-leaved parsley,
  chopped
225 g/8 oz feta cheese, roughly crumbled
salt and freshly ground black pepper
2 avocados, peeled and sliced

- Heat the olive oil in a saucepan. Add the chilli, garlic and shallots and sauté for 3 minutes. Add the vinegar to the pan and simmer until it has evaporated.
- Place all of the remaining ingredients, apart from the avocado slices, in a bowl. Add the garlic mixture and stir well. Leave to marinate for half an hour. Transfer to a portable container and garnish with slices of avocado.

Bulgur wheat salad with peas   serves 4

magic ingredient... peas

Peas contain high levels of vitamin C, which helps the body to absorb iron. If your body lacks sufficient levels of vitamin C, iron will remain in your gut, increasing your risk of developing iron-deficiency anaemia.

1 large onion, finely chopped
2 cloves garlic, finely chopped
2 tablespoons olive oil
450 g/1 lb bulgur wheat
1 teaspoon allspice
450 g/1 lb cherry tomatoes, preferably yellow and orange
2 teaspoons tomato purée
1 teaspoon sugar
salt and freshly ground black pepper
350 ml/12 fl oz water
8 bite-sized florets of broccoli
110 g/4 oz frozen peas
2 medium-sized aubergines, cut into small cubes
2 tablespoons fresh parsley, chopped
1 lime, cut into wedges

- Sauté onion and garlic in dash of olive oil until soft and slightly golden brown. Add the bulgur wheat and stir. Add the allspice, cherry tomatoes, tomato purée, sugar and a little salt and pepper, along with the water. Stir well to make sure that spices are mixed with the wheat. Cover and simmer for 8 minutes.
- Add broccoli florets, cover and simmer for another 4 minutes. Add peas and cook for a further 3 minutes. (You should find that all of the liquid will be absorbed, but the mixture shouldn't become too dry – add a little more water if this is the case).
- Remove from the heat and allow it to rest for 10 minutes with the lid on. Meanwhile, sauté the aubergine cubes in 1 teaspoon of olive oil until soft and golden brown. Drain them on kitchen towel to remove some of the excess oil. Add to the bulgur wheat mixture, along with the parsley, and stir well.
- Serve warm or cold, along with wedges of lime.

Sardine & roasted pepper flan   serves 6–8

magic ingredient... sardines

Sardines are rich in omega-3 and omega-6 fatty acids, two beneficial fish oils that play an active role in preventing heart disease by keeping up the level of 'good' cholesterol in the body.

450 g/1 lb red, yellow or green peppers (or a mixture)
275 g/10 oz white or wholemeal shortcrust pastry (see page 94)
50 g/2 oz butter
50 ml/2 fl oz dry white wine
½ teaspoon salt
6 plum tomatoes, thickly sliced
2 large eggs
150 ml/5 fl oz milk
2–3 tablespoons wholegrain mustard
75 g/3 oz Compte cheese or a strong, mature Cheddar, grated
120 g/5 oz tin sardines in oil, drained, cut in half lengthwise and spines removed
salt and freshly ground black pepper

- Preheat the grill to a high heat. Roast the peppers under the grill, turning them occasionally, until their skins are charred, and then place them in a plastic bag and seal it. Leave the peppers to cool (this enables the skins to be removed easily). When they are cool enough to handle, remove the skins and cut them into medium-sized slices.
- Preheat the oven to 190°C/375°F/gas mark 5.
- Roll out the pastry and line a 22 cm/9 in flan tin. Line the pastry with baking parchment or greaseproof paper, fill it with baking beans and bake in the oven for 8 to 10 minutes, or until the pastry starts to lose its wetness and turns a pale golden brown colour. Take the tin out of the oven and remove the paper and baking beans.
- Melt the butter in a saucepan, add the peppers, wine and salt, cover and simmer for 5 minutes. Add the tomatoes and stir them in well. Cook for 5 minutes and then leave to cool.
- In a bowl, beat the eggs, then stir in the milk, mustard and cheese. Mash the sardines and fold them into the egg mixture. Stir in the pepper sauce, mix well and season to taste (remember that the sardines are salty).
- Pour the filling into the pastry case and bake in the oven for about 30 minutes, or until the flan is golden brown.

Left: Sardine and roasted pepper flan

Stuffed vegetables   serves 4

magic ingredient... vegetables

Vegetables are rich in fibre, which provides feelings of satiety. Ensuring that your fibre intake is high means that your stomach will send plenty of 'I'm full' signals to the brain, which will help to keep your weight down.

2 courgettes, about 15 cm/6 in long
4 baby aubergines
4 large ceps or mushrooms
4 tomatoes, blanched, skinned, cut in half and de-seeded
salt and freshly ground black pepper

Filling for courgettes
40 g/1½ oz green lentils
2 shallots, finely chopped
2 cloves garlic, finely chopped
1 tablespoon olive oil
1 tomato, blanched, de-seeded and diced
handful of basil, torn
1 tablespoon red wine

Filling for aubergines
400 g/14 oz mature spinach, stems removed, chopped finely
50 g/2 oz butter
100 g/3½ oz soft, rindless goats' cheese

Cep or mushroom stuffing
knob of butter
1 sprig rosemary, leaves removed and chopped
handful of parsley, chopped
40 g/1½ oz breadcrumbs

Coriander pesto and tomato stuffing
30 g/1½ oz coriander
200 ml/8 fl oz olive oil
juice of 1 lemon
1 fat clove garlic, peeled and finely chopped
50 g/2 oz pine nuts, toasted in a frying pan
175 g/6 oz mashed potatoes

Couscous
50 g/2 oz couscous per person
150 ml/5 fl oz boiling vegetable stock
handful of parsley, chopped
dash of olive oil
juice of 1 lemon

- Preheat the oven to 180°C/350°F/gas mark 4.
- Lightly cook the whole courgettes in boiling water for 5 to 10 minutes, or until they are tender. Roast the aubergines in the oven for 20 minutes and the ceps or mushrooms for 10 minutes.
- Top and tail the courgettes and aubergines and slice them in half horizontally, cutting diagonally. Remove the seeds with an apple-corer or paring knife and leave the aubergines to drain. Stand the other vegetables with their cut sides uppermost and set them aside.
- To make the filling for the courgettes, cook the lentils in boiling water for 30 to 40 minutes, or until tender, and then drain. Sauté the shallots and garlic in the olive oil. Add the lentils and the rest of the ingredients. Mix thoroughly, season to taste and fill the halved courgettes with the lentil mixture.
- To make the filling for the aubergines, sauté the spinach in the butter for 5 minutes. Mash in the goats' cheese, season and spoon the filling into the halved roasted aubergines.
- To make the cep or mushroom stuffing, first separate the stems of the roasted ceps or mushrooms from the caps. Chop the stems and then sauté them in butter with the rosemary, parsley and breadcrumbs. Season and then stuff the ceps or mushrooms with the breadcrumb mixture.
- To make the coriander pesto, blend the coriander, olive oil, lemon juice and garlic in a mortar and pestle or food processor. Add the toasted pine nuts last, blending the mixture into a lumpy purée.
- Mash a generous teaspoon of the coriander pesto into the mashed potatoes, taste and add more pesto if required. Season and fill the de-seeded tomatoes with the stuffing.
- Pour the couscous into a bowl, cover it with the boiling stock and seal the bowl with plastic film. Leave the couscous to steam for 15 minutes, or until it has absorbed the stock. Fold the chopped parsley into the couscous and shape into a mound on a serving dish. Arrange the vegetables around the couscous. Drizzle the couscous with the olive oil and lemon juice. Either cover the serving dish in plastic film for transportation, or transfer helpings of couscous and vegetables to a rigid container.

Smoked salmon wraps   serves 2

magic ingredient... smoked salmon

Salmon contains linoleic acid, a nerve-repairing nutrient. These wraps are
therefore a good snack for people who have multiple sclerosis.

50 g/2 oz smoked salmon, sliced
1 ripe avocado, peeled, stoned and sliced
handful of rocket leaves
2 flat breads, warmed and cut in half lengthwise
freshly ground black pepper
juice of 1 lemon
2 sprigs fresh dill, chopped

- Arrange slices of the smoked salmon and avocado as well as some rocket leaves on the flat breads. Grind some freshly ground black pepper over the top and drizzle with lemon juice.
- Sprinkle with fresh dill and roll up the flat breads. Cut in half before wrapping in clingfilm.

Tuna niçoise wraps   serves 4

magic ingredient... tuna

Tuna is rich in beneficial fish oils whose anti-inflammatory properties can
ease the pain of rheumatoid arthritis. Cooking the French beans for only a
few minutes before plunging them into cold water enables them to retain
all of their nutrients as well as their fresh bright green colour.

100 g/3½ oz fine French beans, trimmed
3 large, vine-ripened plum tomatoes, roughly chopped
25 g/1 oz anchovies, drained and finely chopped
2 tablespoon black Kalamata olives, stoned and chopped
3 large hard-boiled eggs, quartered
2 cloves garlic, finely chopped
200 g/7 oz tin tuna, drained
4 Cos lettuce leaves, torn into bite-sized pieces
2 tablespoons olive oil
1 tablespoon red wine vinegar
salt and freshly ground black pepper
4 warmed slices flat or pitta bread, cut in half lengthwise

- Blanch the French beans in boiling water for a couple of minutes, then plunge into cold water, drain well and allow them to dry.
- Combine the French beans, plum tomatoes, anchovies, olives, eggs, garlic, tuna and lettuce leaves in a mixing bowl. Add the olive oil and vinegar and toss lightly. Season to taste.
- Place a little of the mixture on each of the slices of flat or pitta bread and roll up carefully.

Tomato & bread salad   serves 4

magic ingredient... tomatoes

Tomatoes are rich in betacarotene, an antioxidant that helps to protect
the body against developing signs of ageing. The bread must be very
crusty, or the salad will be rather soggy. It would be ideal if you could
buy small, sweet, Lebanese cucumbers — if not, use an ordinary cucumber.

350 g/12 oz crusty bread, cubed
8 plum tomatoes, cored, de-seeded and chopped
2 small cucumbers, cubed
1 medium-sized red onion, finely chopped
2 cloves garlic, finely chopped
25 g/1 oz fresh parsley, chopped
2 tablespoons olive oil
1 tablespoon red wine vinegar
salt and freshly ground black pepper

- Preheat the oven to 200°C/400°F/gas mark 6.
- Spread the bread cubes over an ungreased Swiss-roll tin and
  bake them in the oven for 10 minutes, or until they are golden
  brown.
- Transfer the bread cubes to a large serving bowl to cool for a
  few minutes. Then combine them with the tomatoes,
  cucumbers, onion, garlic and parsley. Pour the olive oil and
  vinegar over the salad ingredients, season to taste and toss
  well. Allow to stand for at least 20 minutes to enable all of the
  flavours to combine and penetrate the bread before either
  serving or transferring the salad to a portable container.

Tomato & basil pasta salad   serves 6

magic ingredient... pasta

The starchy pasta contained in this dish encourages the body to produce
relaxing hormones that help you to unwind if you are having to endure a
stressful journey.

2 tablespoons olive oil, plus a little extra
450 g/1 lb uncooked pasta shapes
900 g/2 lb ripe plum tomatoes, de-seeded and coarsely
   chopped
25 g/1 oz fresh basil, finely torn
1 clove garlic, finely chopped
salt and freshly ground black pepper

- Bring a large pan of slightly salted water to the boil, add a little
  olive oil and then the pasta. Cook for 7 to 10 minutes, or until
  the pasta is *al dente*. Drain the pasta, transfer it to a bowl and
  allow it to cool to room temperature.
- Combine the tomatoes, basil, garlic and a little salt and pepper
  with the pasta. Toss well, adding a little more olive oil as you
  do so.

Left: Tomato and bread salad

Peanut butter flapjacks   makes 8

magic ingredient... Oats

Oats contain high levels of biotin, which plays an important role in
building up healthy hair. In addition, peanuts are full of protein, which,
when mixed with the oats in this recipe, provide the body with a slow,
but sustainable release of energy. These flapjacks will provide a good mid-
afternoon energy boost to keep you going until your evening meal.

225 g/8 oz butter
50 g/2 oz brown sugar
50 g/2 oz runny honey
50 g/2 oz unsalted peanuts
50 g/2 oz crunchy peanut butter
350 g/12 oz porridge oats
25 g/1 oz flaked almonds

• Preheat the oven to 150°C/300°F/gas mark 2.
• Melt the butter in a saucepan and add the sugar, honey,
  peanuts and peanut butter. Cook for 1 minute.
• Remove the mixture from the heat and mix in the oats. Turn
  the mixture into a greased 25 x 15 cm/10 x 6 in tin and press it
  down firmly. Sprinkle the flaked almonds over the top. Bake in
  the oven for 20 to 30 minutes, or until the flapjacks are pale
  gold in colour. Leave to cool for 10 minutes before cutting into
  rectangles.

Peach & orange smoothie   makes 1 large or 2 small glasses

magic ingredient... oranges

Oranges are rich in vitamin C, which has been proven to provide
protection against infections like the common cold, to which you can
easily be exposed while travelling. Pour the smoothie into a thermos flask
to enjoy while you are on the move.

4 peaches, stones removed
2 oranges, peeled and pips removed

• Place the fruit in a liquidiser and blend until smooth. If you like,
  you could add a couple of tablespoons of natural yoghurt, milk
  or fromage frais to the smoothie.

Lemon prunes   serves 6

magic ingredient... prunes

Prunes are rich in magnesium, a mineral that assists the body to regulate its temperature, making this dish ideal if you are flying. This dish can be kept covered in the fridge for at least a week, which means that you can make it well in advance of your journey.

450 g/1 lb prunes, stoned and diced
1 lemon, thinly sliced
boiling water, enough to cover the prunes

• Place the prunes and lemon slices in a heatproof bowl. Pour over the boiling water and cover the bowl. Leave to cool at room temperature before transferring to a rigid, sealable, plastic container.

Baked apples stuffed with pine kernels & sultanas   serves 6

magic ingredient... dried fruits

The dried fruits contained in this dish are rich in iron, which helps the body to maintain healthy blood and muscles. Baked apples are particularly good for children. You could either serve them hot with custard, or leave to cool before placing them in a plastic box ready for transportation.

6 large baking apples, such as Bramleys
3 tablespoons pine kernels
3 tablespoons walnut pieces
2 tablespoons chopped dates
75 g/3 oz sultanas
2 tablespoons runny honey
475 ml/16 fl oz apple juice

• Preheat the oven to 180°C/350°F/gas mark 4.
• Core the apples with an apple-corer and remove the pips. Taking each apple in turn, cut a line around its circumference about two-thirds of the way up, just deep enough to cut through the skin, to stop the apple from bursting during cooking. Arrange the apples in a ceramic baking dish.
• Blend the pine kernels, walnut pieces, dates, sultanas and honey in a food processor until the mixture is smooth. Using a teaspoon, pack this mixture into each of the apple cavities, allowing a little to pop out of the top. Pour the apple juice over the apples, cover the dish and bake in the oven for 20 minutes.
• Remove the lid and bake for a further 20 minutes, or until the apples are fluffy.

recipe

solutions

7

Recipes to try in order to alleviate headaches and migraines

Banana and peanut butter slices

Porridge with honey and apple purée

Jerusalem artichoke soup

Meatballs in a rich tomato and vegetable sauce

Pasta with mascarpone cheese, garlic and wild mushrooms

Tuscan bean stew

Summer pudding

Poached cherries

headaches &
migraines

There are a number of nutritional ways to fend off debilitating headaches and migraines.

- Top up your intake of fibre-containing foods. Fibre helps to cushion the hormonal swings that may cause or aggravate headaches and migraines.
- Drink 2 to 3 litres (4 to 5 pints) of water throughout the day. Water assists the fibre to perform its therapeutic function.
- Eat plenty of fruit and wholegrain foods. The natural sugars that they contain are released slowly, thereby raising your blood-sugar level gradually (violent swings in your blood-sugar level often cause headaches and migraines).
- Opt for less acidic fruits such as pears, rather than citrus fruits, which can aggravate headaches and migraines.
- Eat small meals regularly to keep your blood-sugar level balanced.
- Remember that caffeine can cause headaches and migraines, so avoid caffeine-containing drinks in favour of refreshing herbal teas. Rosemary essential oil can also help to relieve headaches and migraines.

Pasta with french beans, broad beans & basil   serves 4

magic ingredient... pasta

By eating pasta you are giving your body carbohydrates that are released gently and slowly into the body, thereby helping to keep your blood-sugar level constant and preventing headaches. Roasted pine nuts make a delicious topping for the pasta without exposing you to the cheese-induced migraines that can be caused by Parmesan.

250 g/9 oz fresh or frozen French beans, trimmed
250 g/9 oz fresh or frozen broad beans
450 g/1 lb fresh pasta shapes
1 medium-sized onion, finely chopped
1 clove garlic, peeled and finely chopped
dash of olive oil
60 g/2¼ oz lean bacon, finely chopped
salt and freshly ground black pepper
handful of fresh basil, torn
handful of roasted pine nuts

- Either steam or boil the French and broad beans until they're *al dente*. Drain well and put to one side.
- Boil the pasta until it is also *al dente* and not too slithery.
- Meanwhile, sauté the onion and garlic in a little olive oil until they have just turned slightly golden brown. Add the bacon and sauté it for a few more minutes, or until it starts to become crispy.
- Toss all of the ingredients together and season to taste. Tear some basil over the pasta and top with roasted pine nuts.

Pear crunch   serves 4

magic ingredient... oats

The oats (and pears) in this recipe provide high levels of fibre, which helps to cushion the absorption of sugar into the blood, making this dish the perfect sweet end to a meal and also one that will ward off energy swings and headaches.

175 g/6 oz dried pears
150 ml/5 fl oz pear juice
6 medium-sized ripe pears, cored and peeled
50 g/2 oz butter
50 g/2 oz light brown sugar
125 g/4 oz porridge oats
1 teaspoon cinnamon
½ teaspoon ground nutmeg

- Preheat the oven to 190°C/375°F/gas mark 5.
- Chop the dried pears into 1.5 cm/½ in pieces.
- Place the pear juice in a small saucepan, along with the dried pears. Bring to the boil and then simmer for 10 minutes, or until the dried pears are soft and tender.
- Chop the fresh pears into bite-sized pieces and place them in a 20 cm/8 in square baking dish.
- Make the topping by first melting the butter in a saucepan. Remove the saucepan from the heat and add the sugar, oats, cinnamon and nutmeg. Stir until the oats are well coated.
- Pour the dried pears and juice over the fresh pears and top with the oat mixture. Bake in the oven for 45 minutes, or until the topping is brown and crisp.

Recipes to try in order to alleviate insomnia

Tomato, goats' cheese and broad bean risotto

Chicken and mushroom savoury crumble

Pasta bows with spring vegetables

Pasta with courgettes and lemon

Tomato and basil pasta salad

Rhubarb and strawberry crumble

Summer fruit bread pudding

Poached fresh figs

insomnia

You may find the following nutritional tips helpful if you are having trouble sleeping.

- If you have supper late in the evening, try not to eat too much, because excess-food-induced indigestion can make you feel uncomfortable and far from sleepy.
- Starchy foods, such as pasta, mashed potatoes and risotto, encourage your body to produce sleep-inducing hormones, so try to base your evening meals around these ingredients.
- Drink camomile (one of the most potent floral remedies for disturbed sleeping patterns) or mint tea at night, rather than caffeine-containing drinks like tea, coffee, hot chocolate and cola-based beverages, and try not to drink such caffeine-rich drinks after midday. Because it stimulates the brain, caffeine adversely affects your ability to sleep well. The ancient Greeks used dill seeds (you will find these in health food shops and supermarkets) to promote sleep; you could try infusing them in water to make a calming drink.
- Although a little alcohol can relax you, too much will disrupt your body's natural sleeping patterns, with the result that you may sleep for longer but will wake up feeling far from refreshed. Excess alcohol can also disrupt your sleep by causing dehydration and drops in your blood-sugar level. So stick to drinking a sensible amount of alcohol and only when your stomach is full.
- Avoid taking vitamin and mineral supplements at night (unless your doctor advises you otherwise), because some supplements, especially vitamin B complex, can stimulate brain activity and thereby prevent you from enjoying a good night's sleep.
- Add a few drops of sleep-promoting herbal and floral essential oils such as basil, camomile and lavender to your bath – they will relax your body wonderfully.
- Try to reduce your stress levels. Exercise often and explore other stress-relieving activities.

Tagliatelle with prawns & spinach   serves 4

magic ingredient... pasta

The pasta in this dish encourages the body to produce sleep-inducing
hormones, making it an excellent, as well as a delicious antidote to
insomnia when eaten early in the evening.

500 g/1 lb 2 oz tagliatelle
1 tablespoon olive oil
16 long-tailed prawns, shelled
1 small glass white wine
1 clove garlic, peeled
6 stalks fresh parsley
50 g/2 oz fresh spinach, stalks removed and shredded
1 tomato, chopped
salt and freshly ground black pepper
Tabasco sauce

- Add the tagliatelle to a large pan of boiling water and boil for a few minutes, until it is *al dente*.
- Heat a dash of olive oil in a pan and add the prawns. Stir well after 3 minutes and then pour in the glass of white wine.
- Heat a dash of olive oil in another pan and add the garlic and parsley. Now add the prawns to this pan, along with the spinach, tomato, a little salt and pepper and a couple of drops of Tabasco sauce. Allow to cook for 3 minutes, then remove the garlic and parsley.
- Drain the tagliatelle (setting a little of the water aside) and add it to the pan containing the prawns. Pour in a little of the pasta water – just enough to thicken the sauce. Wait for 2 minutes and then serve in a hot soup dish.

Roast pears with figs & ginger   serves 6

magic ingredient... figs

Figs provide a source of high fibre, slow release sugar that, when eaten in
the evening, will prevent violent, sleep-disturbing mood swings, leaving
you feeling refreshed when you wake up in the morning.

12 Comice pears, peeled and sliced
12 dried figs, chopped
1.5 cm/½ in piece fresh root ginger, peeled and finely chopped
150 g/5 oz Demerara sugar
150 ml/5 fl oz freshly squeezed orange juice

- Preheat the oven to 180°C/350°F/gas mark 4.
- Combine all of the ingredients in a mixing bowl and then transfer the mixture to a roasting dish.
- Bake in the oven for 20 to 25 minutes, or until the pears are soft and golden brown.

Recipes to try in order to alleviate swings in energy levels

Chicken Caesar salad

Chicken soup with dim sum

Carpaccio

Lentil casserole

Meatballs in a rich tomato and vegetable sauce

Strawberries with balsamic vinegar

Summer pudding

Poached fresh figs

swings in blood sugar & energy levels

Swings in your blood-sugar and energy levels can seriously affect both your mood and performance. If you experience such swings, try taking the following measures.

- Although it may be tempting to reach for foods that contain 'quick-fix' sugars, they will only make the problem worse. Chocolate and other sweet foods cause your blood-sugar level to rise quickly, which stimulates the pancreas to produce insulin, the hormone that rapidly brings it down again. Fresh fruits give the best slow-release, energy boost, so increase your fruit intake.
- Eat plenty of protein-rich foods, including cheese, eggs, fish and chicken, especially for lunch, if you find that late afternoon is when your blood-sugar and energy levels crash. These foods will enable your body to control its blood-sugar levels more effectively.
- Eat plenty of chromium-rich foods, such as cheese, shellfish, baked beans and wholemeal products. Chromium helps your body overcome symptoms of hypoglycaemia (low blood sugar).
- Make sure that you drink plenty of water throughout the day to enable all of the energising vitamins, minerals and slow-release sugars in the food that you eat to be absorbed by your body. Adults should aim to drink 2 to 3 litres (4 to 5 pints) of water a day.
- Only drink alcohol when your stomach is full. Because alcohol is absorbed so quickly it causes the blood-sugar level to drop. The presence of food in the stomach slows down the rate of absorption, thereby lessening blood-sugar swings.
- If you are a smoker, try to give up. Nicotine inhibits the body's production of insulin and glucagon, both hormones that maintain a constant blood-sugar level.

Chicken & avocado wrap   makes 1

magic ingredient...chicken

Chicken contains lean protein, which will help your body to regulate its
blood-sugar level, as well as boosting your energy levels and improving
your mood. It also lasts well in lunchtime sandwiches.

1 slice flat bread
crunchy grain mustard (quantity optional)
2 crispy, green lettuce leaves
1 ripe tomato, sliced
1 breast or leg of roast chicken, cooked and sliced
½ ripe avocado, sliced and drizzled with a little lemon juice
freshly ground black pepper

- Spread the flat bread with a little mustard. Place a lettuce leaf
  or two, and then the tomato, chicken and avocado slices on
  the bread and roll it up. Season with a little freshly ground
  black pepper. Cut the wrap in half before eating it.

Poached cherries   serves 6

magic ingredient...cherries

Cherries contain high levels of carotenes, powerful antioxidant nutrients,
as well as fibre, which slows down the release of fructose into the body
and stabilises the body's blood-sugar level.

225 g/8 oz white sugar
600 ml/1 pint Italian red wine, preferably Chianti or Sappan
1 cinnamon stick
900 g/2 lb cherries, stems and stones removed

- Combine the sugar, wine and cinnamon stick in a large, non-
  aluminium, heavy-bottomed pan. Place the pan over a medium
  heat and stir until the sugar has completely dissolved. Add the
  cherries, lower the heat and simmer gently for approximately
  10 minutes.
- Using a slotted spoon, transfer the cherries to a large serving
  bowl. Cook the remaining juice over a high heat to reduce it
  until it is thick and syrupy.
- Remove the cinnamon stick and pour the syrup over the
  cherries. Allow to cool to room temperature and then chill
  before serving.

Recipes to try in order to alleviate constipation

Roasted peppers and tomatoes

Rosemary vegetables

Chickpea and feta cheese salad

Brown soda bread

Stuffed vegetables

Rhubarb and strawberry crumble

Baked apples stuffed with pine kernels and sultanas

Lemon prunes

constipation

If you suffer from constipation, the following tips should help to kick-start your bowel.

- Ensure that your intake of fibre is high, because fibre in the presence of water forms a soft stool, which stimulates the gut to contract. Pulses, wholegrain foods, fruits and vegetables all contain fibre, and you should therefore try to eat at least five pieces of fresh fruit or servings of vegetables every day, as well as some wholegrain foods, oats and pulses. This may seem a lot, but remember that one option is to make fresh juice from four pieces of fruit for an achievable and tempting fibre boost.
- Make sure that you drink plenty of water every day to assist the fibre in food to stimulate your gut. Adults should aim to drink 2 to 3 litres (4 to 5 pints) a day – about a glass of water an hour.
- Try a glass of prune or fig juice or a compote made of dried prunes or figs. These fruits have a particularly good bowel-stimulating effect.
- Although small doses of caffeine stimulate the small muscles of the intestine to contract (which can alleviate short-term constipation), too much caffeine dehydrates the body. Dehydration makes constipation worse, so try not to drink more than 2 or 3 cups of caffeine-containing drinks a day.
- Exercise regularly to tone up your body, including your bowel muscles. Aim to take twenty minutes of aerobic exercise (walking, swimming, running and cycling) three times a week.
- Keep a food diary to discover whether certain foods, such as dairy products, aggravate your constipation. Removing them from your diet for a couple of weeks should tell you whether you are intolerant of, or allergic to them. If you think that this is the case, seek professional advice to ascertain whether your diet is well balanced.

Warm spicy dahl   serves 4

magic ingredient... lentils

The lentils in this dish provide an excellent form of gut stimulating fibre
and also provide a useful form of protein, making this a nutritious and
constipation-relieving recipe.

225 g/8 oz Puy lentils
1.2 litres/2 pints water
1 teaspoon ground turmeric
1 cm/½ in piece fresh root ginger, peeled and grated
1 clove garlic, crushed
½ teaspoon garam masala
1 teaspoon ground cumin
salt and freshly ground black pepper
2 tablespoons olive oil
½ teaspoon cumin seeds

- Wash the lentils and place them in a large saucepan, along with the water. Bring to the boil and then add the turmeric and ginger. Simmer the lentils for about 40 minutes, or until they are soft.
- Add the garlic, garam masala and cumin, stir and season to taste.
- Purée half of the dahl mixture with the olive oil and then add it to the other half to make a really creamy dish. Stir in the cumin seeds and season to taste.

Date & bramley apple tart   serves 6

magic ingredient... dates

Dates, as well as apples, contain high levels of gut-stimulating fibre.
Remember to drink plenty of water with this dessert to enable the fibre
to do its job efficiently.

basic shortcrust pastry (see page 94)
700 g/1½ lb Bramley apples, peeled and sliced
50 g/2 oz caster sugar
juice of ½ lemon
25 g/1 oz butter
250 g/9 oz Majool or whole dates, stoned and sliced in half
grated zest and juice of 1 orange
150 ml/5 fl oz double cream
25 g/1 oz Demerara sugar
25 g/1 oz flaked almonds

- Preheat the oven to 200°C/400°F/gas mark 6. Place the dough in the flan ring then chill for 45 minutes. Put a piece of greaseproof paper on top of the flan dough and cover it with baking beans. Bake for 20 minutes, then remove the greaseproof paper and baking beans. Return the flan to the oven for about 5 minutes, or until the edges are golden brown and the base has hardened. Set to one side.
- Mix the apple slices with the sugar and lemon juice. Melt the butter in a large pan and add the apples, cooking gently until the apples start to soften and the butter and sugar caramelise.
- Remove the apples with a slotted spoon and place in the pastry case. Arrange the dates on top of the apples. Place the orange zest and juice in the pan with the apple syrup and cook for 25 to 30 minutes, until the juice becomes a thick syrup. Remove from the heat and add the double cream, stirring continuously. When the cream mixture has thickened slightly, spoon it over the apples and sprinkle some Demerara sugar and flaked almonds over the top. Place the tart under a hot grill for 2 to 3 minutes, or until the almonds have started to turn brown.

Recipes to try in order to alleviate depression

Sea bass and crab

Cranberry zester

Blackcurrant cake

Date and orange cake

Apricot and oat honey muffins

Roasted red mullet

Noodles with red peppers, shallots, chicken and cashew nuts

Chicken baked in spicy yoghurt

depression

Although it cannot cure depression, food can help enhance your mood. If you're feeling down, follow some of these guidelines.

- Make sure that you eat lots of lean protein, which contains tryptophan and L-phenylalanine, substances that encourage the brain to produce the endorphins serotonin and noradrenaline (happy hormones).
- Monitor your intake of sugary foods. Although they may result in your brain producing short bursts of endorphins, the sugar swings that they cause usually trigger mood crashes. Try not to eat sugary foods until your stomach contains fibre-rich foods such as vegetables, pulses and wholegrains, as fibre suppresses rapid increases in your blood-sugar level and hence mood swings.
- Ensure that you eat plenty of fresh fruit (at least four pieces a day), because fruit contains slow-release sugars, which can lift and sustain your mood.
- Try to eat as much fresh produce as possible. It contains high levels of vitamins and minerals, the nutrients required to maintain a healthy body and mind.
- Drink enough water to help your body to absorb the beneficial nutrients in food. Adults should have 2 to 3 litres (4 to 5 pints) of water a day.
- Don't drink too many caffeine-containing drinks. Not only can caffeine adversely affect your mood and energy levels, but it can also inhibit your body's absorption of the beneficial nutrients in food. Keep your intake of such drinks to a maximum of three cups a day.

Shellfish casserole   serves 4

magic ingredient... shellfish

Shellfish is rich in zinc, so not only will this dish help to increase your
libido, but because it also contains protein it will stimulate your brain to
produce the 'happy hormones' L-phenylalanine and tryptophan.

200 g/7 oz winkles
800 g/1 lb 11 oz each of mussels, clams and cockles
4 spider crabs, or any small crab, cut in half
300 ml/10 fl oz dry cider
2 shallots, finely chopped
1 clove garlic, sliced
salt and white pepper
1 bay leaf
1 sprig thyme
1 cucumber
1 tablespoon fresh chervil or flat-leaved parsley, finely chopped

- Scrub and wash the shellfish and crabs and place them in a casserole dish with the cider, shallots, garlic, salt, pepper, bay leaf and thyme.
- Cut the cucumber into 16 pieces. Remove and discard the seeds. Add the cucumber to the casserole.
- Place the dish over a high heat and bring to the boil. Cover and cook for 8 minutes, until the mussels and clams start to open.
- To serve, bring the casserole directly to the table. Divide the shellfish between individual soup dishes, cover them with the shellfish juice and sprinkle with the finely chopped chervil or parsley.

Cherries dipped in chocolate   serves 4

magic ingredient... cherries

The cherries will help your brain to produce the mood-enhancing
hormones serotonin and noradrenaline. They also contain high levels of
potassium, a mineral that helps prevent and correct high blood pressure.

20 firm ripe cherries with stems intact
300 g/10½ oz good quality plain eating chocolate, broken into
   small even-sized pieces

- Carefully wash and dry the cherries, making sure to leave the stems intact.
- Break the chocolate into a heatproof bowl that can sit on top of a saucepan, so that the bottom of the bowl does not touch the water below.
- Pour boiling water into a saucepan, then place the heatproof bowl containing the chocolate pieces over the water, making sure that the bottom of the bowl does not come in contact with the water.
- Stir the chocolate as it melts to ensure a smooth and even consistency.
- Remove the bowl from pan once the chocolate has melted.
- Holding a cherry by its stem, dip into the chocolate, submerging the fruit half way. Allow the excess chocolate to drip off and place the cherry on baking parchment to set.
- Work quickly through all the cherries before the chocolate begins to solidify. Make sure that no water remains on the cherries before dipping.

Recipes to try in order to alleviate a low sex drive

Banana and pineapple energising fruit drink

Asparagus and lemon salad

Prawn and Emmental salad

Sea bream in a saffron and ginger sauce

Peach and orange smoothie

Shellfish casserole

Grapefruit and orange mousse

Blackberry and blueberry fool

low sex drive

If you feel that your sex drive isn't as high as it should be, follow these libido-boosting nutritional strategies.

- Eat plenty of fresh food and cut back on fast food – if you have a healthy, well-nourished body, rather than an over-tired, drained one, you are far more likely to have a happy sex life.
- Make sure that your diet is rich in zinc, because low levels of zinc in the body can result in a low libido, along with low sperm counts in men. Foods rich in zinc include seafood, wholegrain bread, green, leafy vegetables, crumbly cheeses and lean red meat.
- Keep your weight within the ideal range for your height and build. If you're happy with your weight you will usually feel sexier, too.
- Monitor your cholesterol level to ensure that it is within the healthy range. Don't follow any cholesterol-lowering crash diets, because these also have the effect of lowering the rate at which your body produces sex hormones. Implement any dietary changes slowly.
- Don't eat too much before having sex – not only will you feel uncomfortable if you have a full stomach, but you will also want to go to sleep, which is clearly not conducive to enjoyable sex.
- Moderate your intake of alcohol. Temporary impotence in men is often due to the anaesthetising effect that alcohol has on the peripheral cutaneous nerves of the penis, while a woman who has drunk too much may not be able to achieve orgasm, let alone be an enthusiastic participant.

Salad of seared prawns   serves 2

magic ingredient... prawns

Prawns are rich in zinc, which does wonders for the libido. They are also
quick and easy to cook, which helps to create a relaxed atmosphere if you
are doing the cooking. This salad is organoleptic, stimulating all the senses.

450 g/1 lb (about 20) tiger prawns, in shells, heads removed
1 clove garlic, finely chopped
salt
dash of olive oil
2 spring onions, finely chopped
1 avocado, stoned, peeled and sliced
12 ripe cherry tomatoes, halved
1 bunch rocket, roughly shredded
400 g/14 oz tin artichoke hearts, drained
2 tablespoons flat-leaved parsley, finely chopped
50 g/2 oz roasted whole almonds
juice of 1 lemon

Dressing
2 tablespoons olive oil
1 tablespoon walnut oil
1 tablespoon lemon juice

- Peel the prawns, make a cut along each of their backs and
  remove the vein. Cut the prawns nearly in half and then press
  flat, into a butterfly shape. Transfer to a grill pan and scatter
  garlic over the top. Season with salt and drizzle a little olive oil
  over the top. Heat the grill to a high heat, but don't cook the
  prawns until everything else is ready.
- Arrange the spring onions, avocado slices and tomatoes on a
  serving plate with the rocket and artichoke hearts. Mix the
  dressing ingredients together and set aside.
- Place the prawns under the hot grill for 2 to 3 minutes, or until
  they become opaque – don't overcook them.
- Arrange the prawns on top of the salad and drizzle the dressing
  over the top. Scatter with the parsley and almonds and sprinkle
  with lemon juice

Raspberry sorbet   serves 6

magic ingredient... raspberries

Raspberries are rich in zinc, a libido-boosting nutrient that also raises
sperm counts in men. In addition, the sensual feel of this delicious sorbet
in the mouth is highly suggestive.

900 g/2 lb fresh or frozen raspberries
275 ml/½ pint water
110 g/4 oz caster sugar
1 teaspoon lemon juice
2 egg whites

- Blend the raspberries in a food processor for a couple of
  minutes to make a purée. Boil the water with the caster sugar
  until the sugar has dissolved. Pour the sugar water into the
  purée, whisk well and allow to cool.
- Add the lemon juice to the purée and pour the mixture into
  ice-cube trays or a shallow freezer container and freeze until it
  is nearly firm.
- Meanwhile, whisk the egg whites until they are stiff, but not
  dry. Transfer the raspberry mixture to a bowl and mash it up a
  little with a fork until it has become a thick, icy mush. Carefully
  fold in the egg whites, return the mixture to the freezer
  container and freeze until firm.

Recipes to try in order to alleviate high cholesterol level

Warmed oatcakes

Mackerel with roasted tomatoes and thyme

Smoked salmon wraps

Creamy prunes

Summer pudding

Pear crunch

high cholesterol level

If you have a high cholesterol level it is vital that you watch what you eat. The following nutritional tips will help you to keep your cholesterol level healthy.

- Eat lots of the foods that produce high-density lipoprotein (HDL), or 'good' cholesterol, like oily fish, garlic, wholegrains, fruits and vegetables.
- Drink 2 to 3 litres (4 to 5 pints) of water a day. Water encourages the fibre in food to swell and stimulates the liver to produce HDL, which carries low-density lipoprotein (LDL), or 'bad' cholesterol, to the gut, from which it is excreted.
- Don't eat too many saturated animal fats. You shouldn't have to avoid them completely, just keep the quantity that you eat down and always accompany them with fibre (team cheese with wholegrain bread and water, for example). Water causes fibre to swell, and the swollen fibre in turn cushions the rate and level at which your body absorbs fat.
- Ensure that your intake of antioxidant-rich foods is high. The nutrients that are present in prunes and other dried and fresh fruits and vegetables, including vitamin C, betacarotene, vitamin E and selenium, help to prevent LDL from being deposited in the blood vessels.
- Remember that drinking a couple of glasses of antioxidant-rich wine a day can not only encourage your body to produce HDL, but the anthrocyanins and other antioxidants that it contains can also play a part in preventing LDL from being deposited in your blood vessels.
- Include garlic in your diet; the allicin it contains inhibits the retention of LDL in the blood vessels.

Tomato, avocado & hazelnut herb salad   serves 4–6

magic ingredient... avocados

The avocados in this salad are rich in vitamin E, a vitamin that helps to prevent heart disease and inhibits LDL or 'bad' cholesterol from being deposited in the blood vessels.

450 g/1 lb vine-ripened tomatoes, blanched and skinned
100 ml/4 fl oz olive oil
25 ml/1 fl oz hazelnut oil
1 tablespoon roasted hazelnuts
1 clove garlic, chopped
juice of 1 lime
1 heaped tablespoon fresh, flat-leaved parsley, chopped
1 heaped tablespoon fresh basil, torn
salt and freshly ground black pepper
2 ripe avocados

- Slice the tomatoes and arrange them in rows on a flat serving dish. Refrigerate until you are nearly ready to serve the salad.
- Make the dressing by first placing the olive and hazelnut oil, hazelnuts, garlic, lime juice, parsley and basil in a blender. Blend for a minute or so, or until the ingredients have been thoroughly mixed. Season to taste.
- Peel, stone and slice the avocados and arrange them on the plate with the tomatoes. Pour the dressing over the avocados and tomatoes and serve at once.

Apricot & cherry oaty pudding   serves 6

magic ingredient... oats

Oats encourage the body to produce HDL, the 'good' form of cholesterol, which helps the body to excrete LDL, or 'bad' cholesterol. Make this pudding in the early summer, when cherries and apricots are abundant.

900 g/2 lb apricots, sliced in half and stones removed
450 g/1 lb cherries, stems and stones removed
50 g/2 oz brown sugar
110 g/4 oz wholemeal flour
25 g/1 oz oats
pinch of salt
2 tablespoons Demerara sugar
50 g/2 oz unsalted butter, chilled and chopped into small pieces

- Preheat the oven to 190°C/375°F/gas mark 5.
- Cut the apricots into large chunks. Place them in a 1.2 litre/2 pint ovenproof dish with the cherries and mix well. Sprinkle the brown sugar over the top.
- Combine the flour, oats, salt and Demerara sugar in a bowl. Add the butter chunks and rub the ingredients together using the tips of your fingers until the mixture resembles breadcrumbs (do not over-mix).
- Sprinkle the oat mixture evenly over the fruit. Place the dish in the oven for approximately 40 minutes, or until the topping is golden brown and the syrup has started to bubble through the edges. Serve while the pudding is still warm.

Recipes to try in order to alleviate anaemia

Marinated oranges

Asparagus and lemon salad

Swiss chard with a lime dressing

Spinach eggy bread

Lentil casserole

Lentil, tomato and pasta soup

Carpaccio

Raspberry fool

anaemia

Many of the symptoms of anaemia, as well as its causes, can be alleviated by taking a few simple nutritional steps.

- First ask your doctor to ascertain whether you have iron-deficiency anaemia (the most common kind of anaemia). If you do, increase your intake of such iron-rich foods as lean red meat, dark-green, leafy vegetables, baked beans, eggs, pulses, liquorice and plain chocolate.
- Make sure that your body is receiving high levels of vitamin C. Eat plenty of citrus fruits and remember that drinking a glass of fresh juice with a meal will help your body to absorb the iron that is contained in the food.
- Drink 2 to 3 litres (4 to 5 pints) of water every day and don't drink too many caffeine-containing drinks, because caffeine inhibits the body's absorption of iron and other beneficial nutrients.
- Moderate your fibre intake, because large amounts of fibre can inhibit your body's ability to absorb iron. Opt for bread made with wheat, rather than wholemeal bread, for example. Because you mustn't decrease your vitamin C intake, however, you shouldn't avoid vegetables and fruits – just keep the amount of bulky, wholegrain-type fibre that you eat to a minimum.
- Make sure that you have plenty of rest and try to reduce your stress levels: your body can't replenish its iron levels if you push it too hard. If you're very anaemic, don't take any vigorous exercise until your body has built up adequate levels of iron and haemoglobin (the iron-rich blood pigment that carries oxygen around the body).

Meatballs in a rich tomato & vegetable sauce   serves 4

magic ingredient... lean red meat

Lean red meat contains high levels of iron, a nutrient that helps correct
iron-deficiency anaemia, nourishes the hair and wards off feelings of
excessive tiredness.

2 aubergines
225 g/8 oz lamb, minced
225 g/8 oz lean pieces of beef steak, trimmed and minced
1 onion, chopped
2 cloves garlic, finely chopped
100 g/3½ oz fresh wholemeal breadcrumbs
1 teaspoon ground allspice
salt and freshly ground black pepper
2 tablespoons olive oil
1 large onion, chopped
1 large aubergine, diced
3 courgettes, sliced
2 large red peppers, chopped
400 g/14 oz tin plum tomatoes
150 ml/5 fl oz tinned tomato juice
2 cloves garlic, finely chopped
1 teaspoon dried oregano
1 teaspoon fresh basil, chopped
1 tablespoon basil leaves, torn

- To make the meatballs, cut the aubergines in half and grill skin side uppermost until the skin begins peeling. When cool enough to handle, peel off the skin with a knife. Chop flesh roughly, then place in a food processor with lamb, beef, onion and garlic. Blend to a fine paste. Add breadcrumbs, allspice, salt and pepper to taste and mix well.
- Divide mixture into eight and shape into balls. Sauté in a dash of olive oil over a medium heat, for about 15 minutes. Transfer them to a plate and keep warm.
- Preheat the oven to 180°C/350°F/gas mark 4. To make the sauce, heat olive oil in a saucepan and sauté the onion and aubergine until softened. Add the courgettes and peppers and sauté, stirring occasionally. Add the tomatoes, tomato juice, garlic, oregano, basil and a little salt and pepper and simmer for 10 minutes.
- Pour the sauce into a large casserole dish. Arrange the meatballs in the sauce, cover and cook in the oven for 20 minutes, or until the sauce is bubbling and the meatballs are piping hot. Garnish with the basil leaves and serve immediately.

Blackberry frozen yoghurt   serves 6

magic ingredient... blackberries

The blackberries contained in this frozen yoghurt are rich in vitamin C, a
powerful antioxidant that helps the body absorb iron and prevents anaemia.

400 g/14 oz fresh blackberries
100 ml/3½ fl oz cold water
200 g/7 oz caster sugar
juice of 2 lemons
300 ml/10 fl oz thick, natural yoghurt

- Purée blackberries with water to make a juice. Sieve juice to remove seeds. Add caster sugar and lemon juice and mix well.
- Fold the yoghurt into the blackberry syrup. Place the mixture in an ice-cream maker and mix for 15 to 20 minutes, until starting to freeze. Transfer to a plastic container and freeze. (If you do not have an ice-cream maker, pour the mixture into a shallow metal or plastic container and put it in the freezer for 2 hours. Remove it from the freezer, beat the frozen edges into the softer centre, then return it to the freezer and leave until it has frozen.)
- Take the frozen yoghurt out of the freezer 5 minutes before you want to serve it to allow it to soften slightly.

the good herb & edible flower guide

Herbs and edible flowers have many healing properties, from the mint that aids digestion and calms a troubled stomach, to the camomile flower that encourages sleep. These curative properties, along with their flavour-enhancing qualities, make them ideal ingredients for my recipes. You will find edible dried flowers in health-food shops, and although you can buy packets of freshly cut herbs in supermarkets

I would encourage you to grow your own, either in pots on the kitchen windowsill, in window boxes, or in a corner of the garden. Because sunlight, heat and moisture can cause their flavours to fade quickly (and they can become mouldy), dried herbs and edible flowers should be stored in small amounts in dark, airtight containers rather than in clear glass pots on herb racks.

Basil
magic property...acts principally on the digestive system, easing wind, stomach cramps, colic and indigestion.

Best used fresh, basil is the perfect partner for tomatoes in salads or sauces, and also enhances the flavour of aubergines and courgettes. It is delicious when combined with garlic in a pesto sauce and complements many pasta dishes. Try it with oily fish such as mackerel, or with roast lamb, chicken, duck and goose.

Bay
magic property...useful for settling disorders of the upper digestive tract and promoting the absorption of food; the essential oil can also ease arthritic aches and pains.

Best dried for culinary purposes, bay leaves impart flavour to pâtés and terrines, as well as baked vegetable dishes, oily fish, goose, pork and veal. Tie up a bay leaf with sprigs of parsley and thyme to make a bouquet garni with which to flavour soups, sauces and casseroles. The essential oil (well diluted in a carrier oil) can be massaged into aching joints.

Camomile
magic property...soothes the body and mind, alleviating stress.

When infused in water, dried camomile flowers make a calming tea.

Chervil
magic property...settles the digestion.

Chervil is best used fresh to complement the flavours of such delicate fish as Dover sole and shellfish. A pretty herb, you can also add it to salads or garnish soup with it. Alternatively, you could chop it roughly and combine it with parsley to make a herb butter to smother over a jacket potato.

Chives
magic property...soothe the digestion.

Possessing as they do a mild, onion-like flavour, chives are usually used in potato salads, egg dishes and delicate cream or butter sauces. Garnish soups and salads with the slender leaves or pink flowers.

Dill
magic property...encourages a good night's sleep, as well as settling the digestion.

Dill is best used fresh, although the seeds as well as the leaves are good for relieving wind and calming the digestion. I use it to flavour salads, sauces, dressings and mayonnaise. It is also a simple, delicious way of enhancing the delicate flavour of poached or baked fish. You could also use it as a garnish for fish soups and pâtés.

Fennel

magic property...having mild diuretic qualities, the seeds help to relieve fluid retention and bloating, as well as soothing away stomach pain and stimulating the appetite.

Three variations on the fennel theme are available to the cook: the feathery leaves, the seeds and the bulb. The leaves make a lovely addition to salads and can also be used to garnish oily fish or roast lamb. The seeds are excellent when used in fish, chicken or roast pork dishes, while the bulb can be roasted.

Garlic

magic property...many health-giving qualities, including reducing the risk of cancer and heart disease, fighting off bacterial infections and reducing catarrh.

Garlic goes particularly well with tomato, fish, lamb and chicken dishes. Vary its taste by either cooking it (for a softer flavour) or using it raw. You can also make garlic butter to serve with bread, baked potatoes or steaks, or else you could use it in salad dressings.

Marjoram

magic property...helps to reduce wind; some people also believe that it soothes headaches.

Although marjoram has a similar flavour to oregano, it is slightly milder. Use it (either fresh or dried) to complement strong-tasting meats, such as lamb or beef, as well as oily fish, game, chicken, tomatoes, courgettes, spinach, eggs and cheese.

Mint

magic property...calms an upset stomach, reduces stomach cramps and relieves bloating.

Many varieties of mint are available; most are best used fresh. Mint enhances the flavours of such vegetables as peas, broad and French beans, tomatoes and potatoes, while freshly made mint sauce is traditionally served with roast lamb and mutton. Use whole mint leaves to decorate desserts or to add to fruit punches and fresh fruit salads.

Parsley

magic property...contains high levels of vitamins and minerals.

Two varieties of parsley are available: the flat-leaved or Italian and the curly-leaved type (which does not have quite as strong a flavour). Use it fresh and in generous quantities. Parsley is traditionally served with fish, in sauces and stuffings, as a garnish, and as an essential part of a bouquet garni (with bay and thyme).

Rosemary

magic property...soothes the digestive system and may also relieve headaches and migraines.

This strong herb, which can be used fresh or dried, combines beautifully with lamb, beef and poultry. Vegetarians use it in pulse and root vegetable dishes.

Sage

magic property...the fresh leaves, when rubbed on to stings and bites, provide a good first-aid measure. The essential oil may regulate periods and also helps reduce hot flushes.

Fresh or dried sage is usually combined with onions in stuffings for pork, duck, goose and chicken. I think that it goes well with such oily fish as herrings and mackerel.

Tarragon

magic property...aids digestion and encourages sleep (it has a mildly sedative effect).

Best used fresh, I frequently combine tarragon with tomatoes, beans, chicken, fish and vegetables. The flavour of quiches and other egg dishes can also be greatly enhanced by tarragon.

Thyme

magic property...when chewed, the leaves can soothe sore throats. Make an infusion to treat muscle cramps, with 25 g/1 oz fresh thyme in 750 ml/25 fl oz water, and put in bath water.

Thyme is a very versatile herb which can be used either fresh or dried in pork, beef, game, chicken, oily fish and beef dishes. Thyme also goes well with potatoes, either sautéd or in a gratin.

index

Index of Recipies

Dedication

For my family. Without your support and
honest critique, I would never have progressed
beyond the mud pies on the outdoor step!

Acknowledgements

The author would like to thank Mum, Dad,
Paul, Laura, Annie, Clive, Tom and Oliver.
She would also like to thank Jim Ainsworth,
Julian Alexander, Tim Atkin, Mike Banks,
Victoria Blackie, Catherine Bradley, Nick Carrell,
Dave Elvin, Jamie Falla, Alex Flower, Dr Katingo
and Anthony Giannoulis, Lyn Graham, Jimmy
Grieves, Andrew and Pam Harrison, Jamie and
Amanda Harrison, Anthony Holmes, Lucy
Holmes, Clare Howarth-Maden, Jess Koppel,
Mark Lucas, Dej Mahoney, Bill Marsen, Tina
Marshall, Eve Mcleod, Polly Melon, Chantal
Michelin, Helen and Johnie Nicholson, Tony
Parker, Kirstan, Kira and Luca T Romano, Lyn
Rutherford, Dr Martin Scurr, Jonathan Shalit,
Dr Sarah Temple, Margaret, Si, Cat and Mark
Vinton, Araminta Whitley, Tamara Williams.

First published in the United Kingdom in 2000 by
Cassell & Co

This paperback edition first published in 2001 by
Cassell Paperbacks, Cassell & Co
Wellington House, 125 Strand
London, WC2R 0BB

A CIP catalogue record for this book is available
from the British Library

ISBN 1841881368

Design style: Parker Williams
Printed and bound in Hong Kong